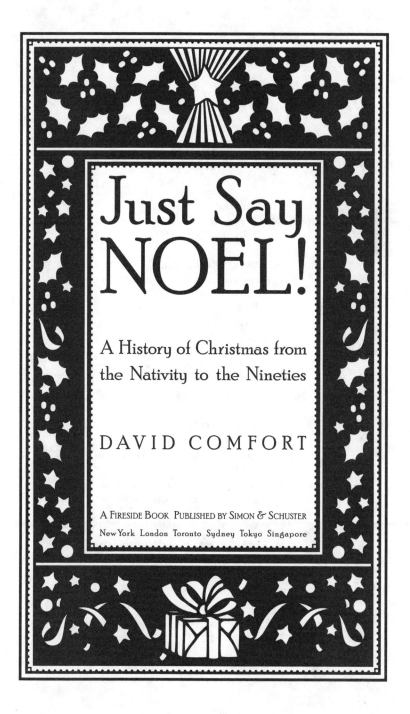

Just Say NOEL!

A History of Christmas from
the Nativity to the Nineties

DAVID COMFORT

A FIRESIDE BOOK PUBLISHED BY SIMON & SCHUSTER
New York London Toronto Sydney Tokyo Singapore

To my mother and father

Fireside
Rockefeller Center
1230 Avenue of the Americas
New York, NY 10020

FIRESIDE and colophon are registered trademarks
of Simon & SchusterInc.

DESIGNED BY BARBARA MARKS

Manufactured in the United States of America

10 9 8 7 6 5 4 3 2 1

Library of Congress Cataloging-in-Publication Data
Comfort, David.
Just say Noel! : a history of Christmas from the nativity
to the nineties / David Comfort.
p.   cm.
1. Christmas~United States~History.   2. United States~Social life
and customs.   I. Title.
GT4986.A1C65   1995
394.2'663~dc20   95-19674
                                                              CIP

ISBN: 0-684-80057-8

Contents

Foreword 11

IV. FRANKINCENSE, MYRRH, & THE MALL

SHOPPING & GIFT-GIVING

VII. NOEL NOIR

**SCROOGES, GRINCHES, ACCOUNTANTS, ECONOMISTS,
AND A FEW ACLU ATTORNEYS**

Foreword

According to a recent national poll, three-quarters of Americans said Christmas was their favorite holiday, nine out of ten celebrate it, and 97 percent exchange gifts. In 1987 we spent $37 billion during the season, in 1994 over $50 billion.

But in another survey, 74 percent said they felt the true meaning of Christmas had been lost, only 2 percent said they caroled, and 25 percent admitted to being down during the holidays. According to a *USA Today* poll, only 16 percent of adults have more fun during the Christmases now than when they were kids—52 percent feel they have less.

So, while holiday spending is up, spirit is alarmingly down.

What gives?

Is America not ready for a spirit rebate?

Just Say Noel! is responding to that need. A seasonal self-helper, a survivalist's stocking stuffer—call it what you will. But it is dedicated to brightening spirits—especially those of the 25 percent who have come down with the holiday humbug, the 98 percent who don't carol, and the growing number who find themselves shopping more and enjoying it less.

How does it propose to do this?

By reporting all the joyful and triumphant tales of Christmases past to present—from the Nativity to the nineties. By mining all its myrrh, frankincense, and gold from the beginning and showcasing it in one modest treasury.

Above all, this text is dedicated to giving the season a much-needed update. A spruce-up, a shine, a makeover. The legends of Christmases past, though near and dear to us, have become a bit dated. What about Christmases present? Many heartening but unheralded events have occurred in recent seasons, providing the stuff for a new generation of Yuletide tales and torchbearers.

Collecting yesterday's holiday highlights and assembling tomorrow's folklore is no small task. The most modern information-gathering means will be used: Nut & Datelines, North Polls, Yule School, and much more.

As we are about to see, Christmastime is a deep well of upbeat and, in many cases, yes, magical information. The more a person, even a slightly grumpy person, learns about it, the cheerier he or she tends to become. Knowledge is power. Ignorance is not bliss. That is the *Just Say Noel!* credo.

Even so, no Santa-like claims and warrantees are expressed or implied here. After getting the bottom line on the Yule in these pages, the reader may not experience an overpowering urge to do some neighborhood caroling. But he or she may find him- or herself delivered from the current humbug epidemic, and surprisingly resistant to it in future seasons.

Now, on that note, all the holiday news and entertainment from the Nativity to the nineties that's fit to print—welcome to *Just Say Noel!*

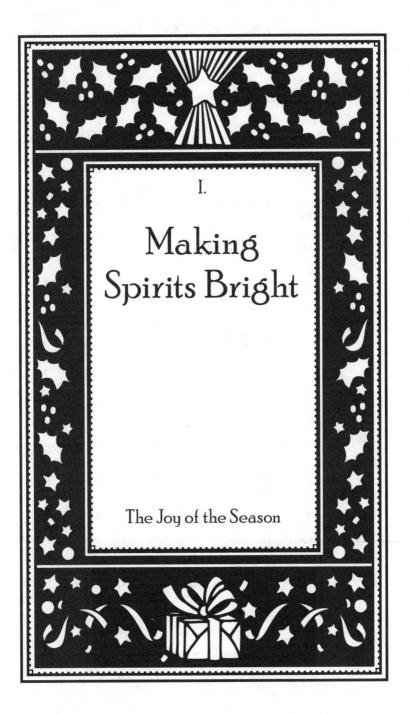

I.

Making Spirits Bright

The Joy of the Season

I will honor Christmas in my heart all the year.

I will live in the Past, Present, and the Future…

Heaven and the Christmas time be praised!

A Merry Christmas to everybody!

A Happy New Year to all the world! Whoop! Hallo!

—Ebenezer Scrooge, after visitations of the three Spirits of Christmas, 1843

I think that if Jesus hadn't been born on Christmas,

my mother would have invented the holiday.

—Mister Rogers, interview for *Ladies' Home Journal*, December 1988

Some memories of a childhood at Christmas time

in Brooklyn: The sound of bells. Bells everywhere.

Wonderful!… Mittens. Yes, I wore mittens a lot.

Not gloves so much. I don't know why.

I guess my mom just loved them. I can still feel them.

I've always loved Christmas!

—Larry King, 1993

A Brief History of Christmas Spirit

Originally Christmas was a Roman winter solstice festivity honoring the sun god, Saturn. The Saturnalia was celebrated annually from December 17 to the 23 and featured feasting, gift-giving, and song. All courts were closed, no one was convicted of a crime, and all men—slave and free, rich and poor—were equal for the week. Romans were governed only by the three laws of the Priest of Cronus during the holiday:

1. All businesses shall be closed except bakeries, cookeries, and those which tend to sport and solace and delight.
2. Anger, resentment, and threats are strictly forbidden.
3. No discourse shall be either composed or delivered, except it be witty and lusty, conducing to mirth and jollity.

These simple regulations laid the groundwork for the Three G's that became the essential ingredients of future Christmas Spirit: Generosity, Gaiety, and Goodwill.

Even so, there was a certain amount of unseasonable behavior between pagans and Christians following the Nativity and during the

Saturnalia-Christmas transitional period. But, as we know, the superior holiday won out in the end, and Pope Julius made this official when he proclaimed the first Yule celebration in 354 A.D.

In the next centuries there were countless conversions, consecrations, and coronations on Christmas Day. In 597 A.D., ten thousand converts were baptized in Kent, England, by missionaries; in 800, Charlemagne was crowned by Pope Leo III; in 1065 Westminster Abbey was consecrated, and so on.

Since that time the spirit of the season has been steadily snowballing worldwide in each of the three G areas—Generosity, Gaiety, and Goodwill—as we see now from our first Nut & Dateline:

521 Camelot: King Arthur and the Knights of the Round Table observe the first recorded English Christmas.

1496 King Henry VII enacts an "anything goes" holiday policy allowing commoners to do anything they want to have fun, including playing cards (which is strictly forbidden the rest of the year).

1543 King Henry VIII takes twenty-one Scottish nobles prisoner at the Battle of Soom Moss, feeds them Christmas dinner, then sets them free. (See "The Turtledove Conquers All," page 37.)

1608 Jamestown, Virginia: Pocahontas rescues Captain John Smith from imprisonment by her father, Chief Powhatan, and the colonists celebrate America's first Christmas. Wrote Smith in his diary: "[We were] never more merrie, nor fedd on more plentie of good oysters, fish, flesh, wild foule and good bread; nor never had better fires in England than in the warm smokie houses."

1836 Alabama is the first state in the Union to declare December 25 a legal holiday.

1843 Charles Dickens writes *A Christmas Carol* in six weeks and it becomes an overnight sensation. At his reading and book-signing in Edinburgh the audience, overcome with holiday spirit, riots. In Glasgow fans storm the platform and try to carry the novelist away. In Boston, New York, and Philadelphia fans stand in line for *Carol* tickets all night in below-freezing temperatures.

1885   Washington: U.S. President Chester Alan Arthur declares Christmas a legal holiday for federal workers.

1942   Bing Crosby cuts Irving Berlin's "White Christmas." It becomes the most popular recording of all time, selling over thirty million copies.

1958   The satellite U.S. *Atlas* transmits a Christmas greeting to the world from President Dwight D. Eisenhower: "To all mankind, America's wish for peace on earth and goodwill toward men everywhere."

1968   Cape Canaveral: NASA workers sneak three bottles of brandy aboard *Apollo 8* as stocking stuffers for astronauts Frank Borman, James Lovell, and Bill Anders on the Christmas moon mission.

1971   Manilla: Philippine President Ferdinand Marcos pardons 327 political prisoners for Christmas. (Nineteen years later, his widow, Imelda Marcos, sends a message to Filipinos saying that when she returns home from exile in Hawaii she will "make it Christmas every day" for everybody.[1])

1975   Los Angeles: The Christmas Doo-Dah Parade premieres. Fifteen years later it is grand-marshaled by Arnold Schwarzenegger, draws a crowd of 65,000, and features fourteen marching bands and twenty floats (including a Mickey Mouse float, a Bart Simpson float, and a Church of Ornamental Lawn Decorators float)—plus Santa himself.

1979   Seattle: The Boeing Company throws the largest Christmas party in history at the 65,000 seat Kingdome; 103,152 people attend.
(For other records, see "Noel Recordbook," pages 89, 115, 161.)

1993   New York: Former "Queen of Mean" Leona Helmsley donates $25,000 to replace Christmas gifts stolen from a Manhattan homeless shelter.
(See "Please Put a Penny in the Old Man's Hat," page 21)

1994   England: Princess Diana and her sons, William and Harry, spend the Yule under the same roof with Prince Charles and

[1]Three years later, on Christmas Eve, the Philippine Justice Department made it Christmas for Mrs. Marcos by clearing her of charges of absconding with $75 million of government funds.

Queen Elizabeth at the family estate in Sandringham. She reportedly has a "pleasant" stay.

1994   Washington: First Lady Hillary Clinton leads reporters on a tour of the Christmas White House. Taking time out to respond to recent unseasonable remarks about her husband's staff from House Speaker Newt Gingrich, she says, "Perhaps we need to be more careful in our treatment of each other. I would hope that the Christmas spirit would take over the heart of everyone."

The
Spirit Stats

F ueled by these joyful and triumphant events in Christmases past, and many others, spirit has been gaining steam over the centuries and today stands at a statistical high.

According to a recent Gallup poll, 90 percent of American adults celebrate the Yule, 1 percent Hanukkah, 4 percent both holidays. And 40 percent of celebrants say Christmas has a "strong" religious meaning for them.[2] But, religious or not, three out of four assert that Christmas is their favorite holiday.

Some other heartening figures:

SEASON'S GREETINGS:
- Number of Season's Greetings cards Americans sent out in 1987: 2.2 billion.
- Number of cards in 1994: 2.6 billion.[3]

---

[2] Thirty-nine percent say it has a "somewhat" religious meaning, 20 percent "not much."

[3] The average weight of a mailman's satchel in December 1994 was 30 pounds; average in July, 15 to 20.

- Percentage of Americans who currently send out cards: 78 percent.
- Average number of cards sent, per household: 26.

CHRISTMAS MAIL:
- Total volume of holiday mail delivered by the U.S. Postal Service, 1983: 10 billion pieces.
- Total volume of holiday mail, 1994: 17 billion pieces.

LONG-DISTANCE PHONE CALLS:
- Average number of calls per day during the 1994 holiday season: 131 million.
- Average number of calls per day, off-season: 54 million.

PARTIES:
- Percentage of companies throwing Christmas parties, 1984: 55 percent.
- Percentage of companies throwing Christmas parties, 1994: 71 percent.

CHARITY:
- Salvation Army Christmas kettle receipts, 1988: $35.6 million.
- Salvation Army Christmas kettle receipts, 1992: $60 million.
- Percentage of Americans who performed acts of charity during the 1993 and 1994 holiday seasons: 82 percent.

Now, how do the numbers translate in terms of real holiday stories of spirit in the three G areas: Generosity, Gaiety, and Goodwill?

Please Put a Penny in the Old Man's Hat: Highlights of Holiday Generosity

The purpose of this is not to show what wonderful human beings we are.

It's to bring holiday cheer.

—Tom Selleck, Christmas Eve, 1993, serving gravy at the Los Angeles Mission,
with Edward Asner, Dean Jones, Laraine Newman, and others

Christmas charity is a subject for volumes in itself. Here is an assortment of highlights from seven centuries, starring generous souls from all walks of life—kings to commoners, presidents to police officers, Santas to strippers, beauticians to Buick salesmen.

LONDON, ENGLAND, 1248: King Henry III has his treasurer fill Westminster Hall with thousands of poor and homeless, and feasts them for the entire Christmas week.

CORNWALL, ENGLAND, 1530: Landowner John Carminow holds a twelve-day Yule open house for "all comers and goers, drinkers, minstrels, and dancers." He serves twelve bullocks, thirty-six sheep, scores of hogs, lambs, and fowl, twenty bushels of wheat, and countless kegs of ale.

MOUNT VERNON, VIRGINIA, 1760–99: George Washington gives each of his ninety slaves a week off for Christmas, plus a bottle of whiskey and twelve shillings.

WALES, 1887: Sir Watkin Williams Wynn throws an open house for five thousand aged and poor. He gives a shilling and a five-pound oxen loin cut to each guest. His wife, Lady Wynn, hands out blankets and flannel.

ASHEVILLE, NORTH CAROLINA, 1905: George Washington Vanderbilt, grandson of railroad baron Commodore Vanderbilt, has a holiday party for the one thousand children of his employees at Biltmore château. He gives them suits, dresses, apples, oranges, and five hundred pounds of candy.

BROUGHTON, ENGLAND, 1971: Peter Curtis runs an ad in the paper offering his seven children to anyone for Christmas. (He says he considers the offer "ideal" for childless couples. His eldest daughter says, "I think he's crazy.")

DARLINGTON, SOUTH CAROLINA, 1979: Raymond Sansbury, a garbage man, is arrested for trespassing when he enters the town dump after hours and collects, as holiday gifts for his seven children, clothing discarded by Mason's Department Store. The next day Sansbury is released on a $200 bond and Mason's invites him and his children to the store to take all the new merchandise they want—free. Later, Sansbury receives $30,000 in cash gifts, including $500 from Sammy Davis, Jr. He buys a $27,500 house, and his life story is optioned by a Hollywood producer for an undisclosed sum.

MICHIGAN, 1984: Postman Frank DePlanche delivers 550 personal Christmas cards to patrons on his rural mail route—but doesn't use stamps. The post office fires him and the case attracts national publicity. Postmaster General William Bolgerafter is deluged with letters of protest from private citizens, U.S. Postal Union members, U.S. congressmen, and DePlanche's wife. Frank DePlanche is reinstated by the Postal Service on the day after Christmas, with apologies.

DETROIT, MICHIGAN, 1988: The female employees at Jason's Strip Club send $24,000 in cash to local Christmas charities.[4]

SINGAPORE AIRPORT, 1989: Singapore Airlines gives away four hundred sleeping bags to passengers stranded due to delayed and canceled holiday flights.

SACRAMENTO, CALIFORNIA, 1993: Local working Santa, Richard Mehlhaff, reports to the Blood Center in his reds for a draw. "I just think it's neat that Santa comes down to do his deliveries and takes time to donate blood," he remarks. Over the years Mehlhaff has given more than fifteen gallons.

TALLAHASSEE, FLORIDA, 1993: On Christmas morning, beautician Johnnie Mosley gives her husband, Charles, her winning lottery ticket worth $15.7 million. Mrs. Mosley had won the lottery in early September, put the ticket in a safe deposit box, and said nothing to her husband. Florida Lottery spokesman Ed George reported, "I don't know of anyone who ever waited this long to cash in." On Christmas, when giving Charles the winning ticket in an envelope with newspaper clippings about the mystery of the unclaimed prize, his wife just said to him, "This is the best I can do this year, honey. I love you."

WORCESTER, MASSACHUSETTS, 1994: At their holiday performance at the Centrum, part of their "Get a Grip World Tour," the rock 'n' roll band Aerosmith gives their manager, Tim Collins, his Christmas present: an $80,000 black Mercedes SL coupe. "I can't believe they did this to me," said Collins. "How can I ever be angry at them now? This is blackmail." The band also collects Toys for Tots gifts from fans redeemable on raffle tickets for seat upgrades and a signed Gibson guitar.

---

[4]The organizations sent the cash back.

PORTLAND, OREGON, 1994: Donning a holly-leaf headdress and a mini Ms. Santa suit with fur trim, Tonya Harding skates to "Have Yourself a Merry Little Christmas" at a shopping mall rink, then passes out candy canes to her fans, wishing them "Merry Christmas" and "Happy Holidays."

Though the Honorable Mention case which follows does not involve shillings, oxen, cards, kids, candy canes, or Mercedes SL coupes, it does feature the holiday ingredient common to all—the spirit of the season.

HONORABLE MENTION

In December 1971, James Paul Harris, a Buick salesman, placed a classified ad in the *Arkansas Democrat:*

WANTED: NEEDY FAMILY FOR SINGLE FATHER AND HIS SON
TO SPEND CHRISTMAS WITH

Harris was divorced and had a nine-year-old son, Ted. His ad was soon being run in newspapers nationwide as a human-interest piece. He received over five hundred cards from all over the country, plus one long-distance phone call from his former wife. She told him she and Tommy, her eighteen-year-old handicapped son by another marriage, were available.

"I decided they were about as destitute as anybody," Harris later reported. "She was out of a job, and the boy was out of the Children's Colony for the holidays. I couldn't find anyone as needy as them."

The two joined James and Ted for Christmas, and wound up staying on—because the Harrises got remarried.

Good Deeds
of
New Yorkers

No warmth could warm, nor wintry weather chill him.

No wind blew bitterer than he, no falling snow or pelting rain was

more intent upon its purpose. The cold within him froze

his features, nipped his pointed nose, shriveled his cheek, stiffened

his walk; made his eyes red and his thin lips blue.

—Charles Dickens, *A Christmas Carol*

We all recognize the chilling description of the famous antagonist.

Though Ebenezer Scrooge was a Londoner, many believe that his successors moved to New York. Over the years, the residents of that city have gained the reputation, if not of actual hard-heartedness, then of being something less than philanthropic at any time of year. But, after examining holiday history, we find that this is a bit of a bum rap.

The giver of the biggest Christmas tip ever, for example, was

James Gordon Bennett, Jr., the publisher of the *New York Herald*. In 1876, the *bon vivant* millionaire had Christmas breakfast downtown at Delmonico's Restaurant, and afterward gave his waiter six $1,000-bills, then left abruptly. Thinking he must not have realized the bills' denomination, the waiter turned the money over to his employer, Mr. Delmonico. When the newspaperman returned to the restaurant days later, Delmonico took him aside and offered to return the cash.

"Why return it?" said Bennett. "Didn't I give it to him?"

"Yes, but of course it was a mistake," stammered the restaurateur. "You gave him six thousand dollars."

"Mr. Delmonico," said his most valued patron, looking him square in the eye, "you should know that James Gordon Bennett never makes a mistake. Merry Christmas!"

A few years later, another eminent New Yorker, J. P. Morgan, began throwing all-you-can-eat Christmas feasts for hundreds of homeless city boys. Though the railroad baron was not always able to attend the festivities personally, the lads never failed to sing "He's a Jolly Good Fellow" in honor of their benefactor.

In future seasons, acts of holiday generosity by New Yorkers were not restricted to tycoons. On Christmas Day in 1965, one Joseph Bonavita threw $10,000 in small bills on the streets of the Lower East Side, creating a stampede. Later, in the early 1980s, a man who would only identify himself as "David the Elf" descended on neighborhood schools in Chinatown, dropped off thousands of dollars' worth of gifts, then disappeared.

The Big Apple seasonal goodwill became contagious. Even a retiring attorney was affected. According to *The New York Times*, in 1990 Harry Lipsig, an eighty-eight-year-old personal-injury specialist, sent sixty thousand holiday cards to everyone he had ever "buttonholed" during his last sixty years of city practice.

Lipsig, of course, was not acting without legal precedent. In the climax of the 1947 holiday classic, *Miracle on 34th Street*, Thomas Mara, the chief prosecutor in the insanity trial of St. Nick, declared:

"Your Honor, the State of New York concedes the existence of Santa Claus!"

It was in the same spirit that the *Times* in 1975[5] asked some

[5]From: "Good Deeds Time: An Unrandom Poll," *The New York Times*, 12-25-75.

notable New Yorkers what good deeds they had done over the holidays. Here are some of the unexpected replies:

On Christmas Eve we invited the Salvation Army band and chorus to sing for the guests and pass the tambourine. It's a forty-one-year tradition here.
—Sheldon Tannen, Vice-president of "21" Club

I gave back the money for my plane fare to Pima County Community College in Tucson, Arizona, where I went to do two days' worth of benefits to raise money for Chicano women who have filed complaints of discrimination.
—Gloria Steinem, Editor, Ms. magazine

My sons call me Scrooge. Santa never visits my house, and the chimney is plugged up . . . But I did do half a deed this year. I helped an old lady halfway across the street at a very busy thoroughfare.
—Zero Mostel, Actor

I tried to be nice to people this week. I smiled at my neighbors and said hello to everybody, which I don't normally do.
—T. H. White, Author

Around Christmas time, I'm just generally very nice.
—Lt. Mary Keefe, Head of NYPD's Sex Crimes Analysis Unit

I have a lot of champagne stored in me. That's a good deed, isn't it?
—Andy Warhol, Artist

Though these remarks were made twenty years ago, the Christmas spirit has not waned even among dyed-in-the-wool New Yorkers. During the 1994 season, former mayoral hopeful Howard "I'll fill every pothole with a convicted murderer" Stern got a jingle from Emilio Bonilla. Stern was on his call-in radio talk show; Bonilla was perched on the scaffolding of the George Washington Bridge with his cellular phone. Stern talked Bonilla down. Days later the radio shock jock donned a Santa suit and held a holiday news conference with the man he saved. "Laughter is the best medicine, and you did it for me," Bonilla told Santa Howard. "You're my hero."

Replied Stern: "You owe me big-time. I expect you to come and paint my house."

Afterward, reporters asked Stern why he did it. Concern? Holiday altruism?

Stern shook his head. "Ratings."

Like Water Closet or Chocolate

It was a chilly evening just before Christmas in Manhattan, 1992. Katharine Hepburn was passing by the Box Tree restaurant, several doors down from her townhouse. Waiters and busboys were picketing outside. The actress stopped at the police barricade and asked Kian Frederick, Restaurant Employees Union organizer, "Aren't you cold?"

"Yeah, a little," he admitted.

"Well," said Ms. Hepburn, "why don't you come to my house to warm up? If any of you have to go to the bathroom or you just want to warm up, come to my house."

Frederick declined the invitation, but thanked her all the same. At that the actress raised her fist, exclaimed, "You beat them!" then continued down the street.

Within the hour she sent her housekeeper back to the Box Tree with two boxes of Christmas chocolates for Frederick and the picketers, and another invitation to use her bathroom if they needed to.

Ladies Dancing and Lords-a-Leaping: A Recap of the Merry Madcap

Having covered Generosity, we now come to the second G of season's spirit—the most infectious and surely the most popular: Gaiety.

During the pre-Christmas Roman Saturnalia, the law required revelers to be jolly, lusty, and gay: it was a misdemeanor to be glum, boring, or nasty. According to record, Roman men made merry by donning gay apparel in the form of animal skins[6] and women's dresses. In the years of the later empire, holiday cross-dressing began to draw sharp remarks of old-fashioned social commentators, such as Caesarius of Arles. "How vile it is that men are clothed in women's skirts," he wrote in the second century A.D., "and *effeminate* their manly strength by taking on the forms of girls, blushing not to clothe their warlike arms in bangles and bows!"

The advent of Christianity did nothing to dampen the playful

---

[6]This holiday tradition was kept alive in Eastern Europe and Scandinavia through the nineteenth century. In Poland and Russia on Christmas Eve at the Festival of the Star, or the Shepherds' Mass, young men often dressed as Bethlehem crèche animals—cows, pigs, and goats. Elsewhere it was popularly believed for centuries that certain men changed into werewolves on Christmas Eve.

seasonal spirit. In the Middle Ages, Christmas celebration was overseen by a royally appointed jester called the Lord of Misrule, the Bishop of Bean, or Abbot of Unreason. He was responsible for organizing all holiday games, pranks, and charades. Clergymen held a dim view of such heathen revelry, and in the seventeenth century the Puritans attempted to outlaw Yule festivity entirely. But the Bishop of Bean always had the last laugh.

Here now, some highlights of holiday merrymaking, century by century, from Camelot to the Clinton White House:

JOUSTING FOR DIAMONDS

(6TH CENTURY)

According to chroniclers, the favorite Christmas recreations at King Arthur's court were, weather permitting: hunting, hawking, wrestling, and jousting for diamonds. Of all the Knights of the Round Table, only Sir Launcelot excused himself from the last activity, because he didn't want to take unfair advantage of inferior sportsmen over the holidays.

STRICTLY BALLROOM

(10TH CENTURY)

Goscelin, a Flemish monk, reported this remarkable Yuletide incident in his popular work, *The Life of St. Edith:* On Christmas Eve, outside the church of St. Magnus in Kolbigk, a group of merry young men and women began to carol and dance, disrupting evening mass. Father Rathbertus hurried out from services and demanded that they stop. They refused, so he called down the wrath of St. Magnus on them. Suddenly the revelers were unable to stop dancing. They continued doing so night and day, under snow and rain, for the next year. Emperor Henry tried to build shelter over them but it collapsed. A survivor of the Christmas dance fever, Othbert, reported that by the following holiday season, just before the spell was broken, "We had trod the earth down to our knees, next to our middles, and at last were dancing in a pit!"

KING HENRY VIII AND HIS MERRY MEN

(14TH–16TH CENTURIES)

The most popular form of Christmas merrymaking in the Middle Ages was mummery—playacting in masks and costumes. In 1348, King Edward III distributed to his Christmas guests at Guildford eighty mummers' masks, mantles with embroidered dragons, and tunics with the heads and wings of peacocks. Nearly two centuries later, Henry VIII and his cabinet dressed up as Robin Hood and the Merry Men and burst in on his first wife, Katherine of Aragon, and her ladies in waiting. The following year, the king dressed up as a peacock and crashed a Christmas party at Cardinal Woolsey's.[7]

HOT COCKLES

(18TH CENTURY)

Later, favorite holiday amusements were parlor games: some for the whole family—Snap Dragon, Blind Man's Buff, Puss in the Corner, Questions and Commands, Hoop and Hide; others for the grown-ups—Hunt the Slipper, Post and Pair, and Hot Cockles. The last was particularly popular. Players would tap a blindfolded person on the shoulder, and he would have to guess their name. At Christmas time in 1711, the *Spectator,* a London newspaper, printed this letter to the advice columnist:

Mr. Spectator, I am a footman in a great family and am in love with the house-maid. We were all at Hot-cockles last night in the hall these holidays; when I lay down and was blinded, she pull'd off her shoe and hit me with the heel such a rap as almost broke my head to pieces! Pray, sir, was this love or spite?

—Signed, "T"

---

[7]A year later, Henry charged Woolsey with treason for failing to get him a divorce from Katherine. The cardinal died just before the holidays.

WHITE HOUSE SANTA

(19TH CENTURY)

By the last century, Christmas mummery was carried on by men dressing up as Santa Clauses. One of the torchbearers of this tradition was President Harrison. On December 22, 1891, the Republican told reporters:

I am an ardent believer in the duty we owe to ourselves as Christians to make merry for children at Christmas time, and we shall have an old-fashioned Christmas tree for the grandchildren upstairs; and I shall be their Santa Claus myself. If my influence goes for aught in this busy world let me hope that my example may be followed in every family in the land.

TYRANNOSAURUS SEX

(20TH CENTURY)

Harrison's political successors have indeed followed his example, and some Democrats have taken things a step further. Senator Edward Kennedy went to the 1993 senate Christmas ball as Barney the Dinosaur, and spent the evening dancing with his new wife, Vicki, who dressed as a Tyrolean girl in a blond braided wig. Explaining his holiday outfit, the senator said, "They don't call me Tyrannosaurus sex for nothing."

ON COMET, ON CUPID, ON CLINTON!

(20TH CENTURY)

"We are pretty crazy in our family about celebrating Christmas," the First Lady has confessed. "The president's a Christmas fanatic like I am." He has played Rudolph the Reindeer in past seasons.[8] "But his

---

[8]According to *The New York Times* ("A White House Christmas," 12-14-93), the president's Rudolph nose and antlers were brought up to Washington by his former next-door neighbor in Little Rock, Carolyn Staley, whom he had recently appointed deputy director of the National Institute for Literacy.

favorite is 'lords-a-leaping,'" she added. During the season, Mrs. Clinton dons Santa Claus red dresses and reindeer accessories; the president Frosty the Snowman and Santa-playing-the-sax ties. In 1993, Chelsea starred as the Favorite Aunt in the Washington Ballet's production of *The Nutcracker*. On the Yule of that year, the First Family, flanked by Secret Service agents, capped off a long day of festivity with a snowball fight on the White House lawn. In 1994, due to recent gunplay at the gates, the family held a "quiet" celebration indoors.

My Most
Favorite Thing

As President Harrison observed, the season's fun is most of all for the kids.

But what is it that youngsters enjoy the most at Christmas time? What's their favorite thing to do? A survey was recently conducted in California on this question, and here's what the kids had to say[9]:

My most favorite thing to do on Christmas morning is to wake up my mom and dad. They usually tell us to get out. Last year my dad had to have his coffee before we could open our presents. It made me happy because he need [sic] to be energized. I love to wake up my mom and dad on Christmas morning. I am going to wake them up until I go to high school. I love Christmas very, very much!
—Augustine Potor, 10, Shingle Springs

I have fun giving my nephews (who are both babies) toys, but mainly, it's giving them—ME! I always make them laugh when they are crying.
—Brittany Johnson, 8, Citrus Heights

[9]From: *Sacramento Bee*, 12-21-93.

When my parents are asleep, I get out of bed. I go downstairs and find a nice place to hide. I bring a camera with me. I bring a sister and a jug of water. If my sister falls asleep I pour water on her. When Santa comes I snap a picture so that the people who don't believe in Santa can see it. I tell my sister to keep her mouth shut. That's my idea of holiday fun.

—Cami Hanson, 9, Shingle Springs

My idea of holiday fun is finding my parents in the act. I hide on the stairs. My parents fill my stocking and wrap my presents without even noticing me. The next morning my brother wakes me up, and starts to bribe me with money. When he is done bribing me we look in our stockings and guess what our presents are, and of course I guess right. After that my brother and I scream at the top of our lungs, "Wake up, it's Christmas!" Christmas is the best time of the year!

—Melanie Bohanna, 9, Fair Oaks

My holiday fun is at 12:05 (A.M.) every Christmas when me and my grandpa and my brothers all get up. We have a big bag of gifts. We go outside. My grandpa holds the gifts, everybody else holds whistles. We go all around the neighborhood dropping gifts on everyone's doorsteps. Then we blow our whistles and run away to the next house.

—Michael Parrish, 10, Rescue

My favorite thing to do is to make cookies. I love putting on the little sprinkles and eating the ones that fall off. The frosting on the angels is very sticky. It tastes good when you lick your fingers.

—Evan Carty, 5, Orangevale

My idea of holiday fun is getting up when it's still real dark and going to the living room where all the presents are, and opening mine. Next, I'll hide them and go back to bed. Then on Christmas morning when everyone gets up, they'll see that I have no presents under the tree. They'll feel sorry for me and buy me new ones, and then I'll have those, plus the ones I opened and hid. That is my idea of holiday fun.

—Paul Scholing, 10, Shingle Springs

The Turtledove Conquers All: Holiday Glasnost, Perestroika, and Global Goodwill

Instead of a real tree, we made a small one from wire coat hangers and green wrapping paper. Yamata enthusiastically joined in and made ornaments from seashells and scrap metal. I particularly remember the large card that he and his friends made, signed and placed on our door. It said, "Merry Christmas, Happy New Year, and sorry about Pearl Harbor."

—Jim Hull, former Army officer, of his holiday in Korea, 1950, with his Japanese houseboys

Having covered Generosity and Gaiety, we now come to our third and most important G: Goodwill.

The last ingredient of Christmas spirit is put hardest to the test in international affairs and wartime. When leading U.S. troops to Europe in 1914, General John "Black Jack" Pershing declared,

"Heaven, Hell, or Hoboken by Christmas!" That holiday sentiment has been shared by many other generals and world leaders over the centuries.

During the holiday season of 1250, King Henry III's chaplain, Peter of Blois, complained: "When you behold our barons and knights going upon a military expedition you see their baggage horses loaded, not with iron but wine, not with lances but cheeses, not with swords but bottles, not with spears but spits. You would imagine they were going to prepare a great feast rather than to make war!" Later, Henry III's successor, Henry V, called time-out in the middle of his invasion of France and the siege of Rouen to serve the enemy Christmas dinner.

Five hundred years after that, on the first Christmas of World War I, English and German soldiers exchanged gifts and brandy, and sang "Silent Night" together between trenches.[10]

In 1974 the Vietcong's negotiating team at Tan Sun Nhut Air Base threw a Yule party for U.S. newsmen, complete with "hardy, scrubbed revolutionary women" singing carols. Similar festivities had been reported seven years earlier by William Tuohy, the *Los Angeles Times'* chief correspondent in Saigon. "During the evening," Tuohy recalled, "Marshal Ky choppered in. He was joined by Vietnamese troops and a busload of choir girls, in flowing *ao dais,* from the city of Hue. Meanwhile, soldiers decorated surrounding barbed wire with colored bunting and affixed paper stars to the tops of sandbagged bunkers. The mood at C-1 had shifted from anxiety to gaiety. Just before midnight, the strains of 'Silent Night' issued from a tape recorder, and a Vietnamese chaplain celebrated midnight mass. Afterward, the post-mass celebration began and GIs broke into a chorus of 'Jingle Bells.'"

The spirit of the season has moved even the most otherwise unyielding dictators. After receiving a deadline from President Bush for unconditional withdrawal from Kuwait, Saddam Hussein wished the U.S. press corps in Baghdad a Merry Christmas and pledged to release POWs. Meanwhile the servicemen of Operation Desert Shield were consuming seventy-five tons of turkey, and their com-

---

[10]The incident was later replayed in the movie *Balalaika,* in which Nelson Eddy sang the carol from his foxhole on the Russian front, and the enemy chimed in.

mander, General Norman Schwarzkopf, to make sure this would not be misinterpreted, declared: "I don't tell the enemy anything. But I will damn sure tell Saddam Hussein that he should not expect us all to be stood down on Christmas and think he's going to be able to catch us napping and asleep on Christmas Day."

Global Goodwill was best expressed on December 25, 1968 by *Apollo* 8 astronauts orbiting the moon. While the first live pictures of earth were televised, William Anders read the Book of Genesis, then Commander Frank Borman concluded, "And from the crew of *Apollo* 8, we close with good night, good luck, a merry Christmas, and God bless all of you on the good earth."

Now some other bright moments of seasons past:

878 During Epiphany Week, King Alfred the Great, at war with the Danes, steals into their camp dressed as a minstrel, and stays there three days playing lute for the enemy.

1551 Edward VI delays the beheading of his uncle, the duke of Somerset, till after the holidays. Reports the king's secretary: "Christmas being thus passed with much mirth and pastime, it was thought now good to proceed with the Duke's execution."

1745 Christmas Day: Austria, Prussia, and Saxony sign the Peace of Dresden, ending the Second Silesian War.

1957 Bob Hope does his Christmas show for seven thousand GIs in Korea's Bayonet Bowl.

1969 John Lennon and Yoko Ono send a holiday message to the world via billboards and full-page newspaper ads: GIVE PEACE A CHANCE.

1972 Coast Guard cutter *Gresham* and Soviet oceanographic vessel *Ernst Krenkel* exchange Christmas gifts off the Maryland coast.

1972 After denouncing "American imperialism," North Vietnamese officer Colonel Nguyen Do Tu, bedecked in red campaign ribbons, apologizes to correspondents for not distributing Christmas cards.

1986 Buddhists and Hindu soldiers of Sri Lanka and Moslem guerrillas of the Liberation Tigers of Tamil Eelam stop fighting for twenty-four hours as a gesture of "Christmas goodwill."

1986   The Embassy of Nicaragua and Lockheed Corporation send
out the same Christmas card.

1988   Lee Iacocca and Honda send out the same card.

1989   Christmas Eve: fugitive Panamanian dictator Manuel A.
Noriega, on the run from former golf partner George Bush, is
granted sanctuary at the Vatican's Panama City Embassy.

1990   President Bush pardons Caspar Weinberger and the Irangate
5, then retires to "Camp Christmas" with Barbara, his fourteen grandchildren, his dogs, and Brent Scowcroft, head of
national security. (Four years later, President Clinton pardons Tom, a fifty-pound turkey, in the Rose Garden. Tom is
retired to Frying Pan Park, in Chantilly, Virginia.)

1990   Saudis prohibit Bob Hope from bringing "his girls," Marie
Osmond and the Pointer Sisters, into their country from
Bahrain to entertain U.S. Desert Shield troops for the Yule.
But they OK his wife, Dolores.[11]

1990   Christmas Day: Salman Rushdie sends a holiday message to
all Islamic nations: "I do not agree with any statement in my
novel, *The Satanic Verses*, uttered by any characters who . . .
reject the divinity of Allah."[12]

1994   Filipino politicians and Roman Catholic El Shaddai officials
put on the largest free Christmas feast ever in Manilla. Five
hundred roast calves and one thousand roast pigs are served
in Rizal Park. Afterward, 230 elderly common-law couples
are married in a Yule midnight mass.

1994   In a Christmas gesture of goodwill from the Central Committee of the Communist Party, Vietnamese Prime Minister
Vo Van Kiet meets with Cardinal Pham Dinh Tung and
praises Roman Catholic contributions to national development.

1994   U.S. troops in Haiti celebrate the Yule with a turkey, ham,

---

[11]Commenting on the restriction the comedian later said, "What bothers me is they
don't want any entertainment—but they still invited me and Dolores."

[12]Though afterward Hesham Essawy, Egyptian chairman of the Islamic Society for the
Promotion of Religious Tolerance, said Rushdie now had a "clean slate," an unseasonable silence from Khomeini fundamentalists indicated that the $1 million bounty on
the author's head was still collectible.

and shrimp feast, interbattalion sports, and a holiday concert by The Kissie Darnell Rhythm & Blues Review.[13]

A final heartening development on the international front involves the Season's Greeting card sent to President Clinton last year by Angel Garcia Seoane, the socialist mayor of Oleiros, Spain. It depicted Fidel Castro as Santa Claus carrying a sack marked "Equality, Brotherhood, and Solidarity!" Said Mayor Angel Seoane: "I want to send a message of peace and goodwill around the world. I've sent one to [Spanish Prime Minister] Felipe Gonzalez and [U.N. leader] Boutros Boutros-Ghali—and to Fidel, of course."

President Clinton's 1994 card depicted a saxophone under the Christmas tree, tea on the table, and Socks the cat lounging at the hearth under three stockings. The message inside read: "Our family wishes you and yours a joyful holiday season and a new year blessed with health, happiness and peace." Some 250,000 cards were sent out. There was no report as to whether Angel Seoane was on the mailing list, or Castro.

---

[13]According to news sources, the following list appeared on a Port-au-Prince command post bulletin board:

YOU KNOW YOU'RE IN HAITI FOR CHRISTMAS WHEN:
- You finally get your Thanksgiving card . . . on Christmas Eve.
- You call home to say, "Honey, I love you. Merry Christmas. Over."
- You get sent home and court-martialed for drinking spiked eggnog on Christmas.
- You decorate the concertina wire instead of a tree.
- Santa gets a letter of reprimand for uniform violations.
- The turkey dinner is a welcome change from the regular diet of lobster, goat, and lamb.

Season's Greetings from the Oval Office

The Sunnyside Museum in Tarrytown, New York (former residence of Washington Irving), is the home of the presidential Christmas card collection. The artwork on the cards reflects the unique spirit of each administration.

What follows is a holiday matchup. On the left is a list of cards from the last nine presidents; on the right—the presidents. The two lists don't match up. Pin each chief executive to his Christmas card.

CARD	PRESIDENT
1. The First Daughter's ducks gliding serenely on the White House pond.	Reagan
2. The First Daughters frolicking in the snow with the First Dogs. (Hint: two are beagles, one is a mixed-breed.)	Kennedy
3. A bucolic nineteenth-century country scene.	Eisenhower
4. A pen-and-ink sketch of the White House.	Ford
5. Portrait of George Washington. (Hint: this card had engraved gold overlays and was mailed in faux velvet envelopes.)	Clinton

6. A festive photo of the Yellow Room with its
   gilded furniture.   Carter
7. A gold-toned Neal Slavin photo of the
   president and First Lady in front of the
   State Dining Room fireplace, with Abraham
   Lincoln's portrait in the background.
   (Hint: on recycled paper.)   Bush
8. The president's own watercolor painting of
   Colorado mountains.   Johnson
9. A Jamie Wyeth night scene of the White
   House. (Hint: only one light burns in the
   windows—the one in the First Lady's
   dressing room.)   Nixon

ANSWER KEY:
1. Kennedy (card from 1961). (In 1962 the card featured a photo
   of Jackie, Caroline, and John John riding in a sleigh drawn by
   their pet pony, Macaroni.)
2. Johnson (1964). (The dogs were Him, Her, and Yuki. The
   daughters were Lynda Bird and Luci Baines.)
3. Ford (1975).
4. Carter (1979).
5. Nixon (1970).
6. Bush (1991). (In 1990 George and Barbara sent a snapshot of
   their Christmas tree; in 1989, it was the decorated South Por-
   tico.)
7. Clinton (1993).
8. Eisenhower (1954).
9. Reagan (1981). (In future years, their cards featured shots of
   White House rooms Nancy restored.)

The Spirit Final

To repeat our Noel credo, where Christmas past and present are concerned, Ignorance is not Bliss. The more one knows the better one feels, until in the end one is myrrhthful and merry by sheer force of glad tidings.

It is in this spirit that we offer the first of seven Noel final exams. The test includes multiple-choice, true-false, and fill-in-the-blank questions on basic Spirit subjects ranging from Dickens' *A Christmas Carol* to the current location of the Wise Men's skulls, to what Moslem queen was the first to throw a three-in-one Yule/Birthday/Anniversary party.

(Double Jeopardy and Extra Credit questions are included for adventurous and advanced students.)

1. When Scrooge first saw the spirit of his dead business partner, Jacob Marley, he refused to believe his eyes because:
   a. He was half asleep and thought he was still dreaming.
   b. He had been drinking.
   c. He was prone to indigestion and thought Marley might be an undigested bit of beef.
   d. He didn't believe in ghosts.

2. The Spirit of Christmas Past was a ————.
   The Spirit of Christmas Present a ————.
   The Spirit of Christmas Future a ————.
   (Briefly describe each, using Dickens' actual words.)
3. What was the main reason Dickens wrote *A Christmas Carol*?
   a. As a protest over the plight of the poor in London.
   b. Money.
   c. Money and fame.
   d. Artistic inspiration.
   e. All of above, but mostly money.
4. The "star" the Wise Men saw en route to the Nativity was Halley's comet. True or false?
5. Legend has it that the skulls of the trio are deposited in the Chapel of the Wise Men in Cologne, Germany. True or false?

DOUBLE JEOPARDY

6. The three Wise Men were in fact:
   a. Zoroastrian astrologers hired by Herod to go East and find out about the bright star there.
   b. Displaced Palestinian camel drivers.
   c. Islamic extremists on the run from a bullion-and-incense heist on the Gaza Strip, and on the lookout for an out-of-the-way Israeli laundering operation.
   d. Ordinary tourists looking for a three-star Bethlehem B&B.
7. In the early Middle Ages, most Christians celebrated Christmas on ————.
8. Name a few old-time Christmas festivals which are celebrated in the U.S. today.
9. Identify two important U.S. Christmas festivals where Santa arrives by dugout canoe.
10. What queen threw the first Christmas party in a Moslem country, celebrated her birthday and wedding anniversary at the same time, and afterward went water-skiing?
11. How many Christmas cards did the Fords send out in 1976? The Reagans in 1983? The Clintons in 1993?
12. According to the *Guinness Book of Records*, the greatest number of Christmas cards ever sent out by a private citizen was:

62,824, by Werner Erhard of San Francisco, California, December 1975. True or false?

13. According to a rural legend from the Old South, on Epiphany night all sheep on the farms knelt in memory of the Child in the manger; cows formed perfect circles; and roosters crowed from sundown till midnight. True or false?

14. In a holiday episode of a popular prime-time TV series last season, a virgin cow—a heifer—gave birth to a baby boy after artificial embryo insemination. Honoring the event, townsfolk put the Nativity statue of the infant Jesus under the statue of a cow. This was the Christmas story from:
   a. *The X-Files*.
   b. *In the Heat of the Night*.
   c. *Picket Fences*.
   d. *Melrose Place*.

EXTRA CREDIT
- In recent holidays, celebrities Leeza Gibbons, Jackie Collins, Mickey Rourke, and Richard Simmons have all sent out Season's Greetings cards with photos of animals. One card showed a Chihuahua; another a Bengal tiger; another six Dalmatians; the last, the star Jack Russell terrier of a hit sitcom. Match the celebrity to the animal.

ANSWER KEY
1. c. He was prone to indigestion and thought Marley might be an undigested bit of beef:
   "*A slight disorder of the stomach makes one's senses cheat,*" Scrooge tells the Ghost of Marley. "*You may be an undigested bit of beef, a blot of mustard, a crumb of cheese, a fragment of an underdone potato. There's more of gravy about you than of the grave!*"
2. Past: "A child-like figure" with a "bright jet of light" springing from his head.
   Present: "A jolly green giant."
   Future: "A draped and hooded Phantom."
3. e. All of above, but mostly money.
   (According to Robert Parks, caretaker of the original *Christmas Carol* manuscript at the J. P. Morgan Library in New York,

Dickens was disappointed with the commercial failure of his earlier novel *Martin Chuzzlewit*, and decided to "write a specific volume about Christmas in order to make money." But, initially, he netted only 130 pounds sterling (about $300) in royalties, spending five times that in legal fees to protect his copyright. By 1845, though, he had earned a quarter million dollars in ticket sales on his U.S. reading tour. [The equivalent of $4 to 5 million today.])

4. False. Halley's comet went over in 11 B.C., well before the birth of Christ. Most current astronomers believe Johannes Kepler's 1604 theory was correct: the "star" was a conjunction of Saturn, Mars, and Jupiter. However, in his January 1992 article in *Sky & Telescope* Rutgers University astronomer Dr. Michael Molnar asserted that the star was in fact the moon eclipsing Jupiter.

5. True. The holy skulls came to Cologne via Constantinople. Constantine the Great's mother was reportedly the original discoverer of the relics.

Double Jeopardy:

6. a. Zoroastrian astrologers hired by Herod to go East and find out about the bright star there.

7. January 6, according to the old Julian calendar. Russians still celebrate the Yule on this day.

8. A Jamestown Christmas
   Williamsburg, Virginia
   The celebration features the "Lord of Misrule," English carols, and Yuletide colonist cookery.
   A Merrie Olde England Christmas Festival
   Boar's Head Inn, Charlottesville, Virginia
   Features medieval feasting, mumming, and music.
   Washington's Delaware Christmas
   Washington Crossing State Park, Titusville, New Jersey
   A reenactment of December 25, 1776, when the general crossed the Delaware with 2,400 soldiers for a Christmas "bash" with British mercenaries.
   Wyatt Earp Christmas Walk
   Monmouth, Illinois

A YMCA-sponsored memorial at the birthplace of the famous lawman, the event features 1800s Father Christmas treats, and attendance by Earp descendants.

Yuletide Yee-haw

Buffalo Bill Historical Center, Cody, Wyoming

Two thousand people turn out for this Old West cowboy ho-ho-down. A Stetson hat replaces the traditional star atop the tree.

9. Donning a red-and-white lava-lava, St. Nick arrives by dugout canoe at Santa comes to Wailea, and at Hawaii Christmas at the Ritz-Carlton, Mauna Lani Hotel.

10. Queen Alia, wife of Jordan's King Hussein Ibn Talal, in 1974. ("But Christmas is not the only reason for the party," she explained. "It is also my birthday and our second wedding anniversary. So we are wrapping three up in one.")

11. Fords: 35,000. Reagans: 75,000. Clintons: 200,000.

12. True.

13. True.

14. c. *Picket Fences.*

Extra Credit:

Leeza Gibbons: Jack Russell terrier, "Frasier's" Eddie, wearing antlers.

Holiday Message: "Dogs who think they're Reindeer . . . On the Next *Leeza.*"

Jackie Collins: Sierra Club photo of a Bengal tiger.

Holiday Message: "Peace on Earth."

Mickey Rourke: His whippet Chihuahua, Angel, held tenderly in his arms.

Holiday Message: "May All Your Dreams Come True! Merry Christmas."

Richard Simmons: His six Dalmatian bitches, on leashes, posing with him in jogging attire.

Holiday Message: "The girls and I wish you pep in your step this holiday season."

II.

Trolling the Yuletide Carol

Christmas Song

With their baudie pipers and thunderying drommers,
they strike up the Devilles Daunce withall, then
marches this heathen companie towardes the church!

—Philip Stubbes, 1575

If I worked behind the counter of a store that played
Christmas music over its loudspeakers, I'd want to be
paid extra for having to listen to it. There are just so many
times anyone can stand to hear "Jingle Bells," "Rudolph,
the Red-Nosed Reindeer," or even "Silent Night."

—Andy Rooney, 1986

We dragged Santa Claus out of the Christmas ghetto
and wrote some really pithy lyrics about him,
like "Jingle Bells, Batman smells" ~kind of a drunken
Christmas party thing, which is more in keeping
with the season. Hey, we're talking somebody's
birthday, for Pete's sake!

—Mojo Nixon, 1993, discussing *Horny Holidays,* which he calls
the "Louie, Louie" of Christmas albums.

A Brief History of the Troll

As we all know, there is no more natural and spontaneous expression of seasonal spirit than in fa-la-la-la-las, chim-chim-cheries, and ve-ni-te a-do-re-muses.

The refrain began more than two thousand years ago with Roman Saturnalia rounds. In the Middle Ages the clergy converted these into devotional chants and hymns. Then the minstrels, balladeers, and folk adapted these into the carols and jingles which enjoy such popularity today.

One of the season's original and most stirring pieces was the *Messiah*, composed by George Frideric Handel in twenty-three days in 1741. At the first benefit performance of the oratorio in Dublin for the Duke of Devonshire, demand for seats was so great that gentlemen were asked to leave their swords at home and ladies to refrain from wearing hoops in their skirts so more people could be seated in the concert hall. Several years later, when the piece was performed for King George II, the English monarch was so moved during the "Hallelujah Chorus" that he rose to his feet, hand to his breast, and the entire audience followed suit. From that day on, it became a tradition to stand during the final movement.

Another holiday immortal is of course Tchaikovsky's *Nut-cracker*. Though it was an immediate public success when presented in 1892, the perfectionist composer was less than completely satisfied with the work. "The piece is far weaker than *Sleeping Beauty*," he declared. "I began the ballet with an effort, sensing a decline in my inventive powers."

Years later, Gene Autry himself wasn't entirely sold on his "Rudolph, the Red-Nosed Reindeer" either. "I thought it was a bit silly with all those reindeer flying around," he confessed to *Country Weekly* magazine in 1994. "But to my surprise my wife, Ina, loved it." Ina's faith was born out. "Rudolph" sold 2.5 million copies the year of its release, 1949, and went on to become the second-biggest holiday hit of all time.

So, in spite of the doubts of certain holiday recording artists, Christmas songs, classic to pop, have never failed to cast their spell on us. In some cases, they have worked actual magic. On Christmas Eve, 1641, St. Joseph of Cupertino was so enraptured when hearing shepherds caroling outside the Church of Grottaglie, in the town of Assisi, he broke into dance, uttered a high-pitched cry, leapt into the air, and *flew* to the altar, where he embraced the tabernacle.

And such miracles are not just a thing of Christmases past. Only last season Perry Como got a sore throat just before he was to go on the air with his "Irish Christmas Special." "I was petrified," the eighty-two-year-old singer later reported. "I thought I wouldn't be able to perform. My wife said, 'Why don't you talk to the Man upstairs?' and I did. I'm pretty Catholic and he's been good to me. I talked to the Fellow—and ten minutes later the sore throat was gone."

The magic continues, and today Christmas music enjoys unprecedented popularity. According to a recent *USA Today* poll, 88 percent of American homes currently play it during the holidays. The average shopper hears nearly one-half of seven hundred continuous Christmas recordings between Thanksgiving and Christmas Eve.

What are the great moments in trolling history which have brought us to this point?

1225 St. Francis and the Franciscans compose the first carols.
1640 First American Christmas song, "The Huron Carol," is written by a French Jesuit in the Huron language.

1870   The crew of the German exploration ship *Germania* holds a carol concert and all-man dance on the North Pole, off the coast of Greenland. The boatswain plays hand organ while the expedition botanist, Dr. Pansch, conducts the chorus. (The group had just finished a Christmas dinner of roast seal and Sicilian wine.)

1892   Tchaikovsky composes *The Nutcracker.*

1946   Spike Jones pens "All I Want for Christmas Is My Two Front Teeth." (For complete rundown of holiday hits, see "Santa Pop," page 58.)

1949   "Here Comes Santa Claus" goes gold. In the next fifty years, the hit is recorded by three hundred artists, and sells 80 million records.

1962   Phil Spector releases his *Wall of Sound* Christmas album, featuring the Ronettes and the Crystals.

1964   *Christmas with the Chipmunks* sells a million.

1965   Lord Douglas Byron releases the first seasonal surf hit: "Surfin' Santa."

1967   José Feliciano cuts "Feliz Navidad."

1970   President Nixon plays piano and the Girl Scouts carol at a White House reception for non-blacklisted journalists and cameramen.

1973   International Society of Santa Claus gives composers Irving Berlin and Joseph Marks the annual Spirit of Christmas Award.

1976   First New York Tuba Christmas concert is played at Rockefeller Plaza featuring a child's symphony of five hundred tubas.

1990   Bob and Dolores Hope sing "White Christmas" for sandbound Desert Shield troops.

1990   First New Wave Cyberpunk Xmas hit, "Hey Lord," by Suicide, a minimalist duo.

1993   Thousands gather at the Chicago Zoo and many other zoos nationwide to sing carols to the inmates.

1993   The Jingle Cats cut a twenty-song CD of carols, *The Meowy Christmas.*

1994   Marine World Africa U.S.A., in Vallejo, California, puts on the "Caroling to the Animals Show." Songs to whales, dolphins, and sea lions include "Deck the Pools with Kelp, Not Holly."

1994   Kenny G, President Clinton's favorite saxophonist, goes triple platinum with *Miracles: The Holiday Album*. The first Christmas album to reach No. 1 since *Mitch Miller's Holiday Sing-Along With Mitch*, 1962, it features "Away in a Manger" and "The Chanukah Song."

1994   Christmas Day: President Clinton, Hillary, and Chelsea sing "Joy to the World" at Foundry United Methodist Church in Washington, D.C.

Top Six Christmas Hits of All Time

"White Christmas"~Bing Crosby

"Rudolph, the Red-Nosed Reindeer"~Gene Autry

"The Little Drummer Boy"~Harry Simeone Chorale

"Jingle Bell Rock"~Bobby Helms

"The Christmas Song"~Nat King Cole

"Santa Baby"~Eartha Kitt

Stille Nacht:
The Story
Behind the
Stanza

Many of our season's favorite tunes came to their creators unexpectedly. Reverend Phillips Brooks' lyrics to "O Little Town of Bethlehem" were inspired by a horseback trip he made from Jerusalem to Bethlehem in 1865. After composing them, he went to Lewis Redner, his organist at the Church of the Holy Trinity in Philadelphia, and asked him to add music. Redner was stumped by the assignment for some time, then he dreamed the melody on Christmas Eve and the next morning wrote the entire score in one sitting.

Nearly a century later, the composition of another holiday classic was as much the fruit of perspiration as inspiration. When Mel Torme and his lyricist composed "The Christmas Song" for Nat King Cole, it was during a summer heat wave in Los Angeles. They wrote "Chestnuts roasting on an open fire . . . Jack Frost nipping at your nose" and the rest in under an hour while consuming cold drinks at the piano and putting ice to their foreheads.

Perhaps the most famous of our Christmas tunes, "Silent Night," came to its composers not as a result of a dream or an L.A. heat wave, but of an unexpected little creature stirring in the night . . .

Late on Christmas Eve, 1817, a mouse chewed through the bellows of the great pipe organ at St. Nicholas Church in Arnsdorf, Austria. The young organist, twenty-four-year-old Father Joseph Mohr, was beside himself. There was no time for repair. A musicless Christmas Mass was unthinkable. He hurried to the house of his friend, Franz Gruber, the local music teacher: together they hastily penned *"Stille Nacht,"* Silent Night.

Hours later at St. Nicholas Christmas Mass, Mohr explained to the assembled congregation that the organ was out of order. Then, before alarm could set in, he and his co-writer performed "Silent Night," he himself playing guitar and singing tenor, Gruber singing bass, the choir backing up with four-part harmony. The new song saved the night for the St. Nicholas parishioners.

In ensuing seasons, the piece was performed by troupes of Tyrolean folk singers. By 1848 it had fallen into obscurity and Father Mohr, then fifty-five, died of pneumonia, penniless. Six years later, however, King Frederick William IV of Prussia heard the song and was so moved he sent his concertmaster out to find its composer. Gruber was discovered.

Santa
Pop

T he transition from the classic holiday tunes of Handel and Tchaikovsky to holiday pop came in 1922 with Ernest Hall's "Santa Claus Hides in the Phonograph." Since that time, Christmas music has proved remarkably adaptable to new genres, and seasonal songs of every kind have made the charts. Here is a rundown of some of the groundbreaking holiday hits in each category—from Oldies but Goodies, to Soul, Surf, and Alternative:

TUNE ARTIST

Oldies But Goodies (1950s)

"Chinchy Old Scrooge"	Phil Moore
"Who Says There Ain't No Santa Claus?"	Ron Holden
"Yulesville"	Kookie Burns

Mambo and Be-Bop

"Mambo Santa Mambo"	The Enchanters
"Be-Bop Santa Claus"	Babs Gonzales

Country
"Grandma Got Run Over by a Reindeer"   Elmo & Patsy
"Christmas on the Range"   Doug Legacy & the
                                        Legends of the West

Soul
"Santa Claus Go Straight to the Ghetto"   James Brown

Surf
"Surfers' Christmas List"   The Surfaris

Blues
"Santa Claus Wants Some Loving"   Mack Rice &
                                        Albert King

Rap
"Christmas at Luke's House"   2 Live Crew

Christian Heavy Metal
"Winter Wonderland"   Stryper

Santa Psycho Pop
"Santa's Elves"   Crash Kills 4
"Santa's on the Nod"   The Grabbers
"Santa Claus Wants Some Lovin'"   Bitch Funky Sex
                                        Machine
"Frosty the Snowman"   Swamp Zombies
"Feliz Navidad"   Manic Hispanic
"Silent Night"   Cisco Poison

Alternative
"Wreck the Halls With Boughs of Holly" The Three Stooges
"Deck the Halls with Boston Charlie"   Lambert, Hendricks
                                        and Ross
"Good King Kong Looked Out"   P.D.Q. Bach
"A Very Merry Chipmunk"   Alvin and the
                                        Chipmunks
"Horny Holidays"   Mojo Nixon
"Santa Claustrophobia"   The Five Chinese
                                        Brothers

Platinum & Gold: The Just Say Noel Top-Five Countdown

HAVE YOURSELF A SCARY LITTLE CHRISTMAS

**ARTIST: JOHN KASSIR, THE CRYPTKEEPER
(FROM *TALES OF THE CRYPT*)**

The Cryptkeeper's holiday CD features: "Deck the Halls with Parts of Charlie," "'Twas the Fright Before Christmas," and "Should Old Cadavers Be Forgot."

"GOOD KING WENCESLAUS"

ARTISTS: THE BUTTHOLE SURFERS

This five-minute limited-edition single features "The Lord Is a Monkey" on the flipside, and includes a video disc with two-headed poodles.

WALKIN' 'ROUND
IN WOMEN'S UNDERWEAR

ARTIST: BOB RIVERS

The double CD holiday set by the Seattle DJ includes "I Am Santa Claus," inspired by the Black Sabbath hit, "I Am Iron Man"; "I Came Upon a Road Kill Deer," a take-off on "It Came Upon a Midnight Clear"; and "The What's-it-to-ya Chorus," an update of "The Hallelujah Chorus." The title cut "Walkin 'Round in Women's Underwear" is a cross-dresser's reinterpretion of "Winter Wonderland." It begins:

> *Lacy things, the wife is missin'*
> *Didn't ask for her permission*
> *I'm wearin' her clothes, her silk pantyhose*
> *Walkin' 'round in women's underwear.*

> *In the store, there's a teddy*
> *With little straps, like spaghetti*
> *It holds me so tight, like handcuffs at night*
> *Walkin' 'round in women's underwear.*

HERE COMES SANTA CLAWS

ARTISTS: THE JINGLE CATS

This is an eighteen-song follow-up to the group's 1993 hit album *Meowy Christmas*. The Jingle Cats are Sprocket, Twizzler, Binky, Cheese Puff, Clara, Cueball, Graymer, Max, and Petunia, owned and directed by Mike Spalla, a thirty-six-year-old video editor from southern California. Spalla accompanies the kitty choir on accordion; his dog, Klippy Kloppy, helps out on vocals. "Here Comes Santa Claws," recorded at Whiskers a Go Go, includes "Fleas Navidad," and reprises Elvis Presley's "Blue Christmas."

THE JINGLE BELLIES
CHRISTMAS ALBUM

ARTISTS: BOBBY BREAUX AND THE POT-BELLIED PIG
Bobby Breaux—former drummer for Woody Herman, Al Hirt, and Ellis Marsalis—collaborated with porcine vocalist, Rebel, a 450-pound boar owned by his friends Dave and Tina Walker of Arlington, Texas. Rebel provided "socially acceptable pig mealtime utterances" on "Greensleeves," "Amazing Grease," and "Hava Nasqueala." Breaux backed the pig up on skins and synthesizer.

Bladder Busting:
*The Nutcracker~*Tennessee Style

In his "Games We Played as Children" (*Tennessee Folklore Society Bulletin,* vol. XII, March 1946), Robert Lassiter tells about his favorite holiday hit sound as a country boy ...

Our unique method for providing some inexpensive musical "guns" was by the use of hog bladders. We always killed five or six hogs at home. The bladders were carefully saved by us children. After these had been well stretched by inflating and deflating and pulling, they were then "blowed" up at the ends, tied and then hung up in some safe place to keep for Christmas. A quill made from the joint of a wild cane, inserted in the neck of the bladder with plenty of breath to blow, did the trick of blowing up . . . On Christmas morning the bladders were taken down and "busted." This "busting" was accomplished by using the back of an axe or by the use of a plank. The noise was really surprisingly loud . . . I'm still wondering why someone did not write a song on "When It's Bladder Busting Time in the Country" and become famous.

Snowin'
in the Wind:
Christmas
Protest Songs

In 1958, before Joan Baez cut "Joe Hill," Donovan "The Ballad of a Crystal Man," or Dylan "Blowin' in the Wind," Stan Freberg came out with "Green Chritma." Radio advertisers protested, forbidding the tune to be played near their spots. The song soon fell into obscurity.

Avoiding Freberg's fate, artists of the 1960s kept things between the lines in such hits as "Frosty the Dopeman" and "The Twelve Drugs of Christmas." Others conveyed their message by singing the old tunes in the right place at the wrong time, the wrong place at the right time, or by refusing to play them at all. In 1966, carolers serenaded HEW chief Sargeant Shriver at home in Washington with protests on the antipoverty program set to "O Come All Ye Faithful," "Hark! The Herald Angels Sing," and "Silent Night." A few seasons later, the Greeks objected when U.S. embassy children from the American Community School in Athens caroled for the dictator, Premier Papadopoulos. In the same year, Simon Parker, a Jewish member of the University of Pennsylvania marching band, refused to perform Christmas carols, was dismissed, and days later reinstated.

Musical protest in the last decade, though still upbeat, has turned more hard-edged. A few seasons ago, Richard Grimley, superintendent of Colchester High School in Vermont, canceled the annual school carol assembly when the glee club announced that it would sing a *Christmas Carol* spoof. Meanwhile, on the West Coast, Culture Clash, a Los Angeles Chicano theater group, put on a holiday musical called *Carpa Clash,* a historical piece set in biblical Palestine: Mary, pregnant, is hiding from Herod and the INS; Joseph, without a Green Card, is on the lam in a border town; and the unborn Jesus' citizenship is in question.

Among the most talked-about musical take-offs from the 1993 season was *Baby Jesus and His Holiday Pixies* from director Benjamin Zook. The Los Angeles production covered everything from the holiday blues, to sex on holiday airplane flights, to the problem of bringing a gay lover home for a family Christmas reunion. Scenes were interspersed with carols by scantily dressed elves. Jesus played backup on an accordion.[1]

[1]From: "Christmas Quirks in Tinseltown, *USA Today,* 12-20-93.

The Hard Nut:
The Nutcracker—New York Style

In 1992 choreographer Mark Morris staged a new production of *The Nutcracker* at Brooklyn Academy of Music Opera House. "This has to be terrifying and grim. Grim and *dangerous!*" he told his dancers during rehearsal.

The former director of dance at Belgium's Theatre Royale de la Monnaie conceived of the *Nutcracker* update several years ago while having a drink at Mort Subite (Sudden Death), a Brussels bar.

The idea behind his *Hard Nut?*

"This is not the shoe-polish, head-patting, candyland view of childhood," Morris pointed out. "That's the way adults think children think, which is always wrong."

The production, instead of being set in the cozy Victorian parlor of the original *Nutcracker*, takes place in a suburban living room of the 1970s. The heroine, little Marie, does not receive a life-size doll or mechanical soldier as in Balanchine's classic, but a life-size remote-control Barbie and a robot. During the dance party, the robot short-circuits and pulls off Barbie's arms.

When asked if he felt *The Hard Nut* might replace *The Nutcracker* as a sentimental seasonal classic, Morris replied, "Why not? That's what I want. Nobody knows a thing about the nineteenth century anymore, and now, well, excuse me, it *is* the late twentieth!"[2]

[2]From: "Mark Morris Likes the Holidays, Really," *New Yorker* magazine, 12-20-93, "Talk of the Town."

Of Carolers, Cocks a Crowing, and the New "Hallelujah Chorus"

1. In the original English version of "The Twelve Days of Christmas" published by J. O. Helliwell in 1842, instead of "ten lords a leaping, nine ladies dancing, eight maids a milking, and seven swans a swimming," the lyric is: "ten cocks a crowing, nine bears a beating, eight hounds a running, and seven squabs a swimming." True or False?

2. On what late-night Christmas TV show was the "Hallelujah Chorus" sung by twelve dummies and ventriloquists?
   a. *Late Show* with David Letterman.
   b. *Late Night* with Conan O'Brien.
   c. *The Tonight Show* with Jay Leno.
   d. *Saturday Night Live*.

3. *Quayle Quayle*
   Knows his grades were bad and reflected gaps in his knowledge
   Quayle Quayle
   Knows his mom and dad got him in the electoral college.
   Who sang this refrain for "What Child Is This?" at the White House Christmas party in 1991?

     a. Mark Russell.

     b. Mojo Nixon.

     c. Murphy Brown.

     d. Washington Steps Comedy Troupe.

4. In Japan the most popular Christmas piece is:

     a. "Little Drummer Boy."

     b. "The Lion Sleeps Tonight."

     c. Beethoven's Ninth.

     d. "We Three Kings of Orient Are."

5. What three artists all recorded "Blue Christmas"?

6. In London, England, 1843, "a young boy gnawed by the hungry cold as bones are gnawed by dogs, stooped down to carol at Scrooge's keyhole." What happened next?

7. In Canton, Ohio, 1974, a ten-year-old girl was wounded by a shotgun blast when the homeowner mistook her for a prowler. What was she actually doing outside his door?

DOUBLE JEOPARDY

8. In the Philippines, 1968, Quezon tribesmen were invited into a house where they killed seven people. Why did the people invite them in?

     a. The tribesmen were dressed as Santa Clauses.

     b. They said they were collecting for the Salvation Army.

     c. They posed as Christmas carolers.

9. *I think everybody was OK until the carolers came through. Then everybody got bummed out. It sank in.*

   Who said this, and under what circumstances?

     a. A survivor from the Quezon incident in the Philippines, 1968.

     b. A spokesman for the Noriega party, hiding from George Bush in the Vatican embassy, Christmas, 1989.

     c. A U.S. service person stationed in Somalia, Christmas, 1992.

10. The first Christmas rap album was recorded by:

     a. Candyman.

     b. Crucial D.

     c. Arrested Development.

     d. Sugarplum Gang and Kurtis Blow.

     e. Snoop Doggy Dog.

11. The first Hawaiian Christmas album was recorded by:
    a. Don Ho.
    b. Jim Nabors.
    c. The Hawaiians with Gesu Bambino.

12. According to Margot Adler, author of *Drawing Down the Moon*, the current population of practicing pagans in the U.S. is 100,000. At a typical present-day pagan Yule celebration, participants sing traditional carols with pagan words, have an energy-raising drumming session, and dance around a Christmas tree. True or false?

13. Name four holiday tunes which have animal first names in their titles.

EXTRA CREDIT

• The Maltese Christmas wind instrument made of inflated dogskin and which represents the shepherds of Bethlehem is called a ———.

ANSWER KEY:

1. True.
2. b. *Late Night* with Conan O'Brien.
3. d. Washington Steps Comedy Troupe.
4. c. Beethoven's Ninth.
5. Hugo Winterhalter, Ernest Tubb, and Elvis Presley.
6. "At the first sound Scrooge seized his ruler with such energy, that the singer fled in terror."
7. Caroling.

Double Jeopardy:

8. c. They posed as Christmas carolers.
9. c. A U.S. service person (Rhonda LeBeau) stationed in Somalia, 1992.
10. d. Sugarplum Gang and Kurtis Blow.
11. c. The Hawaiians with Gesu Bambino—*Christmas Aloha*.
12. True, according to Janet Christian, president of Bay Area Pagan Assemblies. Other covens and wicca groups also invoke the powers of the four directions, and perform a solar child mystery play.

13. "Randolph, the Rouge-Nosed Reindeer," "Dominic, the Italian Christmas Donkey," "Harvey, the Christmas Hippo," and "Rubber Legs, the Knock-Kneed Christmas Monkey."

Extra Credit:
- Tambour , or Zakk.

Noel
Name-That-Tune
Final

This concluding carol quiz is for graduate-level Yule Schoolers:

1. The first German Christmas carol composed in the year 1050 was "Susser Trost, mein Jesus kommt." True or false?
2. "Another Lonely Christmas" appeared on the B-side of Prince's 1988 holiday single. What was on the A-side?
3. What Santa oldie-but-goodie has been recorded 300 times, generating sales of more than 80 million records?
   a. "Dig That Crazy Santa Claus," by Oscar McLollie.
   b. "Here Comes Santa Claus," by Gene Autry.
   c. "I'm Gonna Lasso Santa Claus," by Brenda Lee.
4. Four hits which ask St. Nick for more than just sugar, spice, and everything nice are ———, ———, ———, and ———.

DOUBLE JEOPARDY
5. Name three country tunes which relate to holiday "drinkin' and messin.'" (Hint: two relate to St. Nick himself.)
6. *It was Christmas in prison and the food was real good.*
   We had turkey and pistols carved out of wood.

This is the first verse of what original country tune?

   a. "Christmas in Jail," by The Youngsters.

   b. "Christmas in Prison," by John Prine.

   c. "Christmas in the Jailhouse, Ain't That a Shame," by Leroy Carr.

7. Name five seventeenth- and eighteenth-century holiday harpsicord tunes.

8. What carol spoof from the 1960s involves the explosion of a rubber cigar?

9. A senior citizen drinks too much eggnog on Christmas Eve, has a mishap, and:

   When they found her Christmas mornin',

   At the scene of the attack,

   There were hoof prints on her forehead,

   And incriminatin' Claus marks on her back.

   Identify this oldie that the Irish Rovers brought back for the 1986 season.

10. *You bet your sweet bippy, Santa's a hippie.*

   This is the chorus of which popular 1960s song?

11. Before becoming San Francisco's top-rated radio personality, Erich "Mancow the Madman" Muller was fired from his DJ job in Kansas City for playing this song on the Yule:

   a. "Christmas Is for Mugs," by Graham Parker.

   b. "Horny Holidays," by Mojo Nixon.

   c. "Rudolph, the Brown-Nosed Reindeer."

12. Last season, Muppets' Kermit the Frog and Gingrich the Newt ("Speaker of the Swamp") sang what carol with Larry King on his holiday show?

EXTRA CREDIT

WHO SAID IT? AND WHAT HOLIDAY HIT IS BEING DISCUSSED?

1. "Scrooge runs a pawn shop, makes all the local musicians hawk their instruments, and hardly pays them at all. Then somebody finds a marijuana cigarette in the gutter and gives it to Scrooge. He changes his tune, throws a party, gives all the instruments back, and has everybody play jazz until the police come and break things up."

2. "It wasn't an easy project to pull together. When I first put headphones on Binky and Cheese Puff, they were sort of freaked. I always hoped they'd understand [Christmas music]. Eventually they did."

3. "Those kind of things I don't get into and we don't play. I like music that's more psychically empowering."

4. "The disc is clean because Christmas is a family time, a holy time."

ANSWER KEY:

1. False. It was "Sys Willekommen Heirre Kerst."
2. "I Would Die for U."
3. b. "Here Comes Santa Claus," by Gene Autry.
4. "(Dear Santa) Send Me a Man for Christmas," by The Weather Girls; "I Want Eddie Fisher for Chrismas," by Spike Jones; plus, "I Want a Beatle for Christmas," and "Santa Bring Me Ringo."

Double Jeopardy:

5. "Daddy's Drinkin Up Our Christmas," by Commander Cody; "Santa Came Home Drunk," by Clyde Lasley and the Cadillac Babies; "Santa's Messin' with the Kid," by Eddie C. Campbell.

6. b. "Christmas in Prison," by John Prine.

7. Louis-Claude Daquin's "Noël en Trio et en Dialogue"; Michel Corrette's "Noel Allemande"; Bach's Cantata No. 151: "Susser Trost, mein Jesus kommt"; Heinrich Schutz' "Christmas Oratorio"; Alessandro Scarlatti's "Cantata Pastorale."

8. "We Three Kings of Orient Are":
   trying to smoke a rubber cigar:
   It was loaded; it exploded—
   We two Kings of Orient are . . .

9. "Grandma Got Run Over By a Reindeer." Originally by Elmo and Patsy.

10. "The Happy Hairy Hippie Santa Claus."

11. c. "Rudolph, the Brown-Nosed Reindeer."[3]

---

[3]Another Mancow seasonal stunt: During the 1993 Christmas rush at San Francisco International Airport, he strung a "Welcome to Chicago" banner at the receiving gates, creating panic among arriving travelers.

12. "Jingle Bells." Kermit was appearing on the King show to plug his holiday album *Kermit—Unpigged* (without Ms. Piggy).

Extra Credit:

1. Music historian Dr. Demento discussing Phil Moore's 1953 hit, "Chinchy Old Scrooge" (which appears on *The Demento Christmas Collection*).
2. Mike Spalla, of the 1993 holiday hit album *Meowy Christmas* by his pop group, The Jingle Cats.
3. Phil Stewart, Muzak's holiday programming director, referring to "Walkin' 'Round in Women's Underwear," an X-rated 1994 version of "Winter Wonderland" by Seattle DJ Bob Rivers.
4. 2 Live Crew's Luther Campbell, of the rap group's 1993 offering *Christmas at Luke's House*.

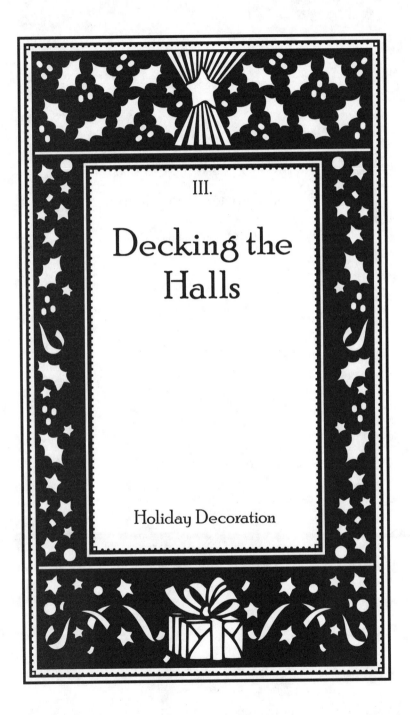

III.

Decking the Halls

Holiday Decoration

The president makes

a great partridge in a pear tree.

—Hillary Clinton, Christmas, 1993

A Brief History of Rosemary, Tinsel, and Thyme

Over the last two thousand years, holiday decorations and decking-the-hall traditions have changed dramatically.

In the year 700, St. Boniface introduced the first Christmas tree by accident. When preaching the Nativity to Druids outside Geismar, the British missionary chopped down an Oak of Wotan to prove that, contrary to the current popular belief, it was not sacred. Falling, the tree crushed all nearby shrubbery except for a fir sapling. So Boniface dubbed it "the Tree of the Eternal Christ Child."

Later, in 1978, James R. Higgins patented the "Artificial Collapsible Xmas Tree," equipped with a telescopic mast and tinsel top. In the same year, Marvin R. Jones developed the "Underwater Christmas Tree." A short time later, Anthony Tengs, a part-time condom designer and chocolatier from Alaska, patented "The Spirit of Christmas," an invisible tree.

The use of mistletoe has also evolved over the ages, along with popular conceptions and misconceptions about it. In 500 B.C., the ancients called the plant *Omnia sanitatem*, believing it to be a cure-all, especially for female infertility. Dionysian cults used large quantities of the evergreen at their annual winter orgy. Centuries later, in 1989 A.D., mistletoe was banned at Moorhead State University after a female instructor filed a grievance, saying it encouraged sexual harassment. The following year, a Los Angeles woman filed a sex discrimination suit after being attacked under mistletoe.

Let's examine a few other historic examples of holiday decoration evolution in our next Nut & Dateline.

THE CHRISTMAS TREE

1539   The first official Christmas tree of the Holy Roman Empire is erected at Strasbourg Cathedral. Villagers from miles around journey to admire it.

▼

1993   A programmer from Cygnus Support, a California computer software company, develops the first "virtual" Christmas tree. "Cyber-Surfers" from coast to coast log on to admire it.

1561   A strict holiday ordinance is passed in Ammerschweier, Alsace, and is posted on signs for all local bankers and merchants to see:
        NO BURGHER SHALL HAVE FOR CHRISTMAS MORE THAN ONE BUSH OF MORE THAN EIGHT SHOES' LENGTH.

▼

1973   Citibank of New York erects a tree on Park Avenue made of three seven-story flagpoles with metal branches and stars bearing Citibank's corporate symbol. Outraged, Tiffany & Co. runs an ad in *The Wall Street Journal* accusing Citibank of "polluting the aesthetic atmosphere of Park Avenue" with its "loud and vulgar" Christmas tree.

MISTLETOE

200 B.C.   The Druids successfully introduce mistletoe at winter fertility fests.

▼

1969 A.D.   Massachusetts Public Health Department urges that kissing under mistletoe be stopped due to the danger of spreading mononucleosis.

1993   Mike Bradford, nineteen, a student of University of California at Santa Barbara, invents the "mistletoe head-dress." He says that since wearing the device, his "kiss success rate" on campus has escalated from 0 to 20 percent. (There is no report of Bradford contracting or spreading mono while using the headdress.)

CHRISTMAS LIGHTS

1520   After marveling at the stars twinkling through evergreens outside his house in Saxony, Martin Luther puts candles on his tree. His neighbors follow suit. A fad is started.

1983   Al Copeland, founder of Popeye's Famous Fried Chicken, New Orleans, installs a 250,000-bulb Christmas display at his house, attracting 500,000 tourists. His neighbors follow with a suit and restraining order which he ignores. The Louisiana Supreme Court tells him to cease and desist with the light show.

(For more recent holiday brown-outs, see "The Kilowatt Kings," page 85.)

1882   Edward Johnson, Thomas Edison's partner, invents electric Christmas tree lights and hangs the first string on his tree.

1973   Due to the energy crisis, Con Ed and President Nixon ask Americans to extinguish all outdoor Christmas lights. The Decorative Lighting Guild of America protests, saying that the request threatens its members with bankruptcy. Days before the Yule, at the urging of congressmen, the president suspends the restriction so Americans can "buoy their morale."

CRÈCHES & BLOW-UP SANTAS

1223 St. Francis of Assisi gets special permission from the pope to set up the world's first Nativity in Greccio, Italy. The display features live barnyard animals and goes over so well with the public that St. Francis reportedly stands by the scene sighing with "unspeakable sweetness."

1985 In a precedent-setting decision, *ACLU v. Village of Scarsdale, New York*, the Supreme Court rules that Nativity scenes on public land violate separation of church and state statutes, unless they conform to "the Reindeer Rule"—a new regulation which calls for equal opportunity of nonreligious symbols such as reindeer. (see "The Crèche and Caroling Wars," page 231.)

1989 The City Council of Paramus, New Jersey, orders a local company to remove a fifteen-foot-tall inflatable Santa Claus and a twenty-foot inflatable reindeer from its roof, saying the decorations violate Paramus building codes.

1994 San Jose's Christmas in the Park Board removes the Baby Jesus from Plaza de Cesar Chavez Park. A statue of the Aztec plumed serpent, Quetzalcoatl, commissioned with $500,000 in public funds, is installed in its place. (In protest, activists form a "living Nativity scene" in the park, complete with angels and a couple dressed as Mary and Joseph.)

Of Trees and Trimming

The centerpiece of holiday decking tradition, the Christmas tree, didn't gain its preeminence until well into the nineteenth century. Its first important populist was Princess Helen of Mecklenburg, who brought a spruce from Germany to France after she married the Duke of Orleans in 1837. Seven years later Prince Albert of Saxony and Queen Victoria trimmed a Scotch pine at Windsor.

In 1856 President Franklin Pierce put up an evergreen at the White House. Five years earlier, Mark Carr, a logger from the Catskills, rented a sidewalk in New York City for a single silver dollar, and established the nation's first Christmas tree lot. Carr did such a brisk trade that the owner of the sidewalk upped his rent to $100 the following season.

The ornament industry was soon keeping pace with the booming tree business. In 1870, the manufacture of lead stars, crosses, butterflies, and diamonds began. In 1878 a company in Nuremberg, Germany, introduced strips of silver foil called "icicles." Two years later, Frank Woolworth went out on a limb and "reluctantly" stocked some blown-glass ornaments in his fourteen stores. By the 1930s, blinking lights had become available. Finally, in 1963, the first polyvinyl chloride, or PVC, Christmas tree hit the market—and all the pieces were now in place.

Today, decking activity and sales stand at an all-time high, as we see from the following statistics and Gallup poll results:

- Percentage of Americans who say they put up a Christmas tree: 85 percent.
- Percentage who wait till Christmas Eve to decorate tree: 4 percent.
- Number of days the average tree stays up: 21.
- Number of trees trimmed in the 1994 season: 72.5 million. (Number of artificial trees: 37 million. Number of real trees: 35.5 million.[1])
- Net earnings of U.S. Christmas tree industry, 1986: $650 million.
  Net earnings, 1994: $1.2 billion.
- Cost of lighting all Christmas trees in U.S., December 1994: $27 million.

[1]America's most popular tree: Scotch pine (36 percent of the national market share). America's second most popular tree: Douglas fir (20 percent market share).

The Kilowatt Kings

I see this as sort of an overlooked art form. These people are artists,

in every sense of the word. They are just as serious as

any painter or sculptor. Not every one is an artist, but there are some

serious people who should be recognized for their work.

—Christina Patoski, author of the photographic collection
Merry Christmas, America: A Front Yard View of the Holidays

As we have seen, ornamentation has snowballed since Martin Luther put the first candle on a tree, and Thomas Edison's partner hung the first electric light string.

Today a new breed of decorator has cropped up: the Kilowatt King—the individual for whom a modest Scotch pine in the den, a Gabriel in the window, or an inflatable Frosty in the yard is only the tip of the iceberg.

The KW Kings live coast to coast. Their electrifying seasonal displays attract thousands, and there is some healthy competitiveness between them. Here are the current American titleholders:

EASTERN DIVISION CHAMP:

MERVIN WHIPPLE

Mervin Whipple, sixty-four, is a justice of the peace and a cemetery superintendent. But he is better known in his hometown of Killingly, Connecticut, as "Mr. Christmas." Since 1967, he has spent more than a half million dollars on his holiday display. "I'm not old enough to drink and I don't smoke," he told *The New York Times* during the 1992 season, "so I've got to put my money somewhere."

Mr. Whipple's display features 60,000 lights; 85 tons of monuments including angels and white spun-steel deer; 312 animated figures such as turn-of-the-century skaters, foxes roasting hot dogs, and Teen-Age Mutant Ninja Turtles; five battery-driven Santas; and his "pride and joy"—a granite chapel where he has performed 1,471 Christmas weddings.

Mervin Whipple gives each visitor to his house a complimentary photo of himself posing in front of his display. As he hands over the picture he often laughs, "Put that under your pillow at night and you'll have nightmares."

WESTERN DIVISION CHAMP:

DOOLEY STITHAM

More than thirty thousand people visit Dooley Stitham's house on Quietwood Drive in Marinwood, California, every holiday season. Stitham, a fifty-eight-year-old pharmaceutical representative who has been working on his displays since 1958, boasts a complete Santa's workshop and elf bunkhouse, a Peanuts train, an E.T. on the roof, and seven separate Yuletide scenes on the front lawn.

He needs two extra power lines from Pacific Gas & Electric Company to run all his lights; plus seventy-five motors and barbecue rotisseries to run his cartoon characters. Still, he doesn't have a volt to spare. "All I know is that I can't use the toaster or I'll blow every-thing," he told the *San Francisco Chronicle* in the 1988 season.

Stitham and his wife (said to be "a dead ringer" for Mrs. Claus) personally greet all visiting children, give each a candy cane, and introduce them to the stuffed, talking Santa Claus on their front porch (who is connected to their son, Scott, upstairs with hidden microphone wires).

Says Stitham of his display, "Nobody's as crazy as I am."

NATIONAL CHAMP:

JENNINGS OSBORNE

Jennings Osborne, also in the pharmaceutical business, doesn't lay claim to being crazier than everybody, but does concede: "I'm a nut." And he confessed to *The New Yorker* in the 1994 season, "If I see something that someone else has that I want, I'm going to want something twice as big."

In 1986, the businessman strung fifty strands of Christmas lights for his wife, Mitzi, and their daughter, Breezy. By 1993, the display at his 22,000-square-foot mansion in Little Rock, Arkansas, had been expanded to include: 3.2 million lights; a 30-foot world globe suspended on a 100-foot pole; a former Rose Bowl Parade calliope tooting Christmas carols; a locomotive driven by Mickey Mouse; 3 Wise Men with camels, 9 reindeer, an 18-foot Santa; and a flashing holiday greeting sign with 6-foot letters which reads: MERRY CHRIST-MAS, HAPPY NEW YEAR!

"All I want to do is take people along on this fantasy with me," says Osborne of his display.

And almost everybody has been happy to join him for the fan-tasy . . . except his neighbors. Arguing that his spectacle caused traffic jams, littering, and public nuisance, they sued Osborne to cease and desist. The businessman (though he has three other local displays— at Little Rock Zoo, Ronald McDonald House, and Hot Springs National Park) refused. After the suit was filed, he also stopped send-ing his neighbors holiday baskets, each of which contained a whole turkey and ham. He now distributes Mont Blanc pens to journalists covering his story.

Last season, the Arkansas Supreme Court ordered the nation's KW king to reduce the size of his display. The judges were deluged with letters of protest from across the U.S.

Determined to protect his First Amendment Rights, Osborne has pledged to take his case to the U.S. Supreme Court. Otherwise, for the 1995 season, he plans more lights, "something with water," and life-size cardboard cutouts of himself, Mitzi, and Breezy so visitors can "have their pictures taken with the Osbornes."

Biggest, Brightest, Beautifulest

Since Christmas is a time of prosperity and plenty, 'tis the season not only to be jolly, but to go jumbo. This particularly applies in the area of trees, floats, and crèches:

NATION'S LARGEST LIVING CHRISTMAS TREE
- "The General Grant," a 4,000-year-old Giant Sequoia in Sangor, California.
- Designated the Nation's Christmas tree in 1926.
- Height: 267 feet. Circumference: 107 feet.

NATION'S SECOND-LARGEST LIVING CHRISTMAS TREE
- A 300-year-old water oak in Wilmington, North Carolina .
- Designated a national monument in 1929.
- Branch spread: 110 feet.
- Decorations: 750 lights, 1000 ornaments, and a crèche below.
- The tree attracted crowds of 10,000 in the 1930s.

NATION'S LARGEST CUT CHRISTMAS TREE
- A Douglas fir at Northgate Shopping Center, Seattle, Washington.
- Erected December 1950.
- Height: 221 feet.

LARGEST CHRISTMAS TREE AT A CAR DEALERSHIP IN NEW JERSEY
- A Norway spruce at Maxon Hyundai in Union, New Jersey.
- Designated the largest Christmas tree in the Northeast by affidavit from Union Mayor, Greg Muller, December 1994.
- Height: 92 feet. Branch spread: 70 feet.
- Decorations: 12,000 lights, and a crèche below.
- Extras: A christening performance by Newark Boys Choir and Garden State Brass Ensemble.

NATION'S LARGEST RELIGIOUS CHRISTMAS LIGHT DISPLAY
- Domino's Pizza World Headquarters, Ann Arbor, Michigan.
- Decorations: 500,000 lights on trees, buildings, and biblical sets. Visitors drive through a 2.5-mile illuminated forest with tunnels lit by beaming angels.
- Extras: Nativity scene with actors portraying Mary, Joseph, and the Wise Men. Shepherds tend live farm animals—sheep, donkeys, and chickens.

LARGEST CHRISTMAS PARADE FLOAT
- "The Merry Christmas, America Float" at the 40th Annual Christmas Parade, Baton Rouge, Louisiana, December 1986.
- Dimensions: 155 feet long, 24 feet wide.
- Features: three double arches, a 17-foot Christmas tree, two 15-foot peppermint candy sticks, and 5,380 feet of wrapping paper.

LARGEST CHRISTMAS DECORATION
- Walt Disney World's Santa Cap atop the "Earffel Tower," part of the Jolly Holiday Christmas Spectacular display.
- Weight: 500 pounds.

Of Partridges, Peanuts, and Presidents

Decorating our own tree is a ritual the president

and Chelsea take very seriously. We are pretty crazy in our family

about celebrating Christmas."

—Hillary Clinton, 1993

As in so many other areas relating to the Yule, our presidents have had a decisive hand in decking traditions. Here now, questions about a few administrations and their trimmings:

1. During the holiday season, George Washington decorated his house at Mount Vernon with:
    a. A large tree cut from the property, decorated with roses, apples, and sugar cookies.
    b. A small potted tree, plus holly, mistletoe, and window Nativity handcrafted by local craftsmen.
    c. A few plain evergreen boughs.

2. Teddy Roosevelt, a conservationist, prohibited Christmas trees in the White House. His boys, Archie and Quentin, spirited one in during the holidays in 1901. When their father discovered the tree he scolded them and had it removed. True or false?

3. Calvin Coolidge was the first president to use electric lights on the White House Christmas tree in the season of 1923. True or false?

4. An hour after the national Christmas tree was presented to President Ford by his home state of Michigan in 1974:
   a. The tree was blown down in a windstorm.
   b. A congressional aide ran over it with his car.
   c. It was set ablaze by an arsonist as a protest against the Nixon pardon.

5. The lights of the national tree in Washington have been reduced or turned off during which three holiday seasons, and why?

6. How much did Christmas light sales decline during the energy crisis of 1973?
   a. 18 percent.
   b. 27 percent.
   c. 92 percent.
   d. Not at all.

7. The 1987 congressional tree-trimming contest was won by Senator Jesse Helms for his tree, which was decorated with peaches, partridges, peanuts, and photos of former president Jimmy Carter. True or false?

8. In honor of "The Year of American Craft," the 1993 White House Christmas tree was decked with more than a thousand ornaments handcrafted by U.S. artists. What were some of the custom ornaments modeled after First Family members?

9. The 1994 holiday decor at the Clinton White House was based on what popular Christmas carol:
   a. "Deck the Halls."
   b. "The Twelve Days of Christmas."
   c. "Jingle Bells."
   d. "O Come, All Ye Faithful."

ANSWER KEY:

1. c. A few plain evergreen boughs. (Christmas trees were not seen in the states until 1830. The first U.S. public exhibition of a Christmas tree took place in York, Pennsylvania. The price of admission: 6¼ cents.)
2. False. He reportedly chuckled, and let the boys keep it.
3. False. It was Grover Cleveland in 1895. (In 1923, Coolidge began the tradition of lighting the national tree on the White House lawn.)
4. b. A congressional aide (Wayne Hose) ran over it with his car.
5. 1973, Nixon Administration—the energy crisis. (The national tree was decorated by a single star at the top, which the president lit on December 14, with the help of a Campfire Girl and a Boy Scout.)

    1979 and 1980, Carter Administration—the Iranian hostage crisis. (The national tree was lit up on Christmas Eve, 1980, for only 417 seconds—one second for each day of the hostages' captivity.)
6. c. 92 percent.
7. False. The creator of this prizewinning tree was Senator Sam Nunn.
8. A Bill angel playing saxophone. A Chelsea angel playing harp. And twenty-one Sockses—Socks pulling Santa's sleigh, Socks playing sax, Secret Service Socks on the roof of the gingerbread White House, and others.
9. b. "The Twelve Days of Christmas." Turtle dove, French hen, partridge, and other theme ornaments adorned each of the fifteen trees in the executive mansion.

Holiday Crèche and Burns

Then comes the ultimate nightmare: getting the tree to fit

into the stand. Performing brain surgery with a hangover is easier.

When you finally get the tree standing on its own, you crawl

out of there with bleeding hands, severe neck and back injuries,

and a desire to choke the very next reindeer you see.

—Lewis Grizzard, "The Joy of Being Single Is No Christmas Tree,"
December 1990

The U.S. Consumer Product Safety Commission keeps a tally of Christmas decoration accidents, based on hospital emergency room records nationwide.

In the last decade the numbers have nearly doubled in all areas. In 1982 there were about 1,000 mishaps involving Christmas tree lights; by 1992 the number had climbed to 3,500. "Non-electric" holiday decoration accidents reached 2,500 in 1982, 3,700 in 1992. Candle accidents: 1,000 in 1982, 3,500 in 1992.

Here are some ER reports from the early 1990s:

- Patient was putting up Christmas lights, lost balance, and fell off roof; fractured humerus.
- Patient's mother states that patient accidentally swallowed Christmas ornament.
- Patient lacerated his tongue while attempting to eat a glass snowman.
- On the way down to the cellar to get Christmas decorations, patient tripped and fell down flight of steps. (Admits to six beers.)
- Patient tore scalp on a nail while putting box of Christmas ornaments away in the attic.
- Patient put Christmas tree ornament in left ear.
- Patient swallowed a jingle bell at school.

Finally, the following unprecedented holiday mishap was reported not by the U.S. Consumer Product Safety Commission, but the international newswire last season:

In Flitcham, England, two twin sisters, Lorraine and Levinia Christmas, were hospitalized after having a head-on crash with one another on an icy country road. The Christmas twins were on their way to each other's house to deliver gifts. Said their mother, Joan Christmas, afterward: "People always say the twins always do things together. It is remarkable they crashed into each other this time of year."

The
Decking Final

1. "Mistletoe" comes from the Greek word *Mista*, meaning "dung," since the plant was originally propagated by seeds in bird droppings. True or false?
2. Due to its pagan roots, mistletoe use was forbidden by the medieval church. What holiday plant did it replace mistletoe with? Why?
3. Christmas trees were first introduced in America by:
   a. French missionaries in the Great Lakes area.
   b. German Hessian mercenaries fighting for George Washington.
   c. The pilgrims of Massachusetts.
   d. The Christianized Mohawk Indians.

DOUBLE JEOPARDY
4. Henry Schwan, a Lutheran pastor of Cleveland, Ohio, was nearly expelled from his parish for putting up a church Christmas tree in 1851. He pleaded his case and saved his career by citing a pro–Christmas tree edict written by a medieval pope. Name that pope.

5. Explain the old German Christmas tradition of the glass pickle ornament.

6. In 1994 the Society of American Florists reported that 56 million poinsettia plants were sold in the U.S. Who brought the original plant from Mexico to the U.S. in 1828?

7. In 1990, the first Rent-a-Christmas-Tree Service was launched in San Diego by:
   a. The Sierra Club of California.
   b. Sierra Pacific of California.
   c. Lloyd R. Johnson of Alpine, California.
   d. Save-a-Tree-Eat-a-Beaver Foundation.

8. Due to Christmas tree poaching along state highways during the holidays, the New York and New Jersey Transportation Departments, as well as many others, spray roadside evergreens with noxious repellents. True or false?

9. In 1979 a man climbed the sixty-five-foot Rockefeller Center Christmas tree and didn't come down for eighty minutes. He was:
   a. A Sierra Club member protesting the harvest of Christmas trees.
   b. A New York maintenance worker replacing burnt-out lights.
   c. An activist protesting the hostage crisis in Iran.
   d. A tourist who wanted a bird's-eye snapshot of the skating rink.

10. What decorations did our servicemen in Somalia improvise for their trees in the 1992 season?

EXTRA CREDIT
- Since the turn of the century the German firm Richard Glaesser G.M.b.H, Inc., has been crafting classic wooden *Nutcracker* soldiers with painted faces and rabbit-fur beards. In 1991 a rival German toy company came out with a new *Nutcracker* soldier which caused Glaesser president Klaus Huebsch to object: "You have to go with the spirit of the times. But these go too far—they're not in keeping with tradition!" What new and nontraditional *Nutcracker* soldiers were Huebsch referring to?

ANSWER KEY:

1. True.
2. Holly. (Its pointed leaves represented the thorns in Christ's crown; its berries, his blood.)
3. b. German Hessian mercenaries fighting for Washington—the same who helped him rout the British at Trenton, after crossing the Delaware on Christmas night.

Double Jeopardy:

4. Pope Gregory I. In 597, the pontiff wrote a letter to Augustine of Canterbury, instructing the missionary to encourage Christmas tree use among the pagans in England as a means of converting them to Christianity.
5. The glass pickle ornament was hung in an out-of-the-way spot on the tree late on Christmas Eve. The first child to find the pickle Christmas morning was given a special gift, and an adult who found the pickle was guaranteed good luck all year.
6. Dr. Joel Roberts Poinsett, the first U.S. ambassador to Mexico.
7. c. Lloyd R. Johnson of Alpine, California. In his maiden season, Johnson rented 1,200 live trees to San Diegans. The fee for a 8-foot Scotch pine was $10, plus a $2 security deposit.
8. True. The New York Deptartment of Transportation started the practice in 1979, using deer repellent. Now many other state departments spray "heat activated" chemicals which are undetectable on a tree outdoors, but indoors, in a heated house, emit (according to *The Wall Street Journal*) a "noxious stench."
9. c. An activist protesting the hostage crisis in Iran.
10. Mosquito netting, ammo casings, instant coffee packets, and GI condoms.

Extra Credit:

- Desert Storm infantrymen in full camo, carrying semiautomatic rifles. These *Nutcrackers* for the nineties were shipped to stores in munitions boxes.

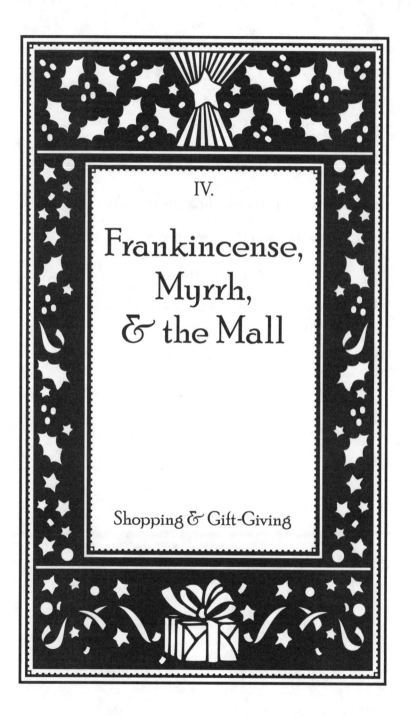

IV.

Frankincense, Myrrh, & the Mall

Shopping & Gift-Giving

The impulse to spend seizes everyone.
He who the whole year through has taken pleasure
in saving and piling up his pence becomes
suddenly extravagant!

—Fourth-century Latin journalist Libanius, on the shopping fever
which traditionally overtook Romans during solstice time

A Brief History of Shopping and Gift-Giving

For the origin of holiday shopping and gift-giving we must again return to the prototype of Christmas, the Roman Saturnalia. Several years before the Nativity, Emperor Augustus had a dream in which citizens gave him gold for the holidays. The next morning, the tyrant—interpreting the dream as a directive from the gods—announced that he and his wife, Agrippina, would accept such donations from Romans on a voluntary basis. If a Roman decided to give—well and good. If a citizen decided not to give—the centurians would simply collect his head after the Yule.

Getting into the holiday spirit, Romans lavished Augustus and Agrippina with gifts that December.

And, not ones to break with tradition, Augustus' successors kept it alive.

Gift-giving has come full circle in two thousand years, many feeling like Roman citizens when venturing into the malls and mail-order catalogs, searching for that special something for the Augustus or Agrippina in their lives.

Otherwise, as our next Nut & Dateline illustrates, the evolution of shopping and gift-giving over the last millennia has turned on four variables: the economy, the taste of the time, the availability or unavailability of discount outlets, and a reliable Santa list.

1099 A.D. Christmas Day: Pope Paschal II gives crusader Baldwin I a crown and the throne of Jerusalem.

1558 Queen Elizabeth I gets a "richly wrought" dress from suitor John Betts; 40 pounds in a red silk purse from admirer Matthew Parker; 75 pounds from the archbishop of York; and 100 pounds from the archbishop of Canterbury. In return she gives everybody dinnerware. (Bloody Mary, her sister in the Tower, gets one dress embroidered with Venetian silver, plus "a fatte goose and a capon.")

1620 Christmas Day: The Pilgrims land on Plymouth Rock and give themselves Massachusetts without consulting the Indians.

1760 George Washington gives his five-year-old stepson, Jackie, and his three-year-old stepdaughter, Patsy: "A bird on Bellows, a Cuckoo, a turnabout Parrot, a neat dress'd Wax Baby."[1]

1864 On Christmas Eve, General William Sherman tells President Lincoln: "I beg to present to you as a Christmas gift the city of Savannah!"

1913 U.S. Congress asks Americans to put Christmas money into war bonds, and considers embargoing all holiday gifts, Tinkertoys and Erector sets in particular. Magnate A. C. Gilbert and toy lobbyists march on Washington with Tinkertoys and Erector sets. Congressman assemble the toys, are impressed, and announce that they've changed their minds.

1971 Vice President Spiro Agnew announces his Christmas gift ideas at a life insurance convention at the Waldorf-Astoria Hotel. For President Nixon (in preparation for meeting Mao), "The complete history of China." For Mao (in preparation for meeting Nixon), "The com-

---

[1]The Christmas mail order is placed September 1759 from London toy shop, Unwin & Wigglesworth; but it does not reach the colonies until the following March.

plete history of the NFL." For Ambassador George
Bush, "A two-place dinner set—so he can entertain all
our friends at the U.N."

1972   For the person who has everything, the Neiman Marcus
holiday catalog offers "You": a talking sculpture of yourself which says "Yes," "No," and laughs on command.
Cost: $3,000, plus airfare for the artist to come to the
customer's home to take facial impressions. (For other
bargains, see "Neiman's Noel," page 119.)

1973   Protesting the commercialization of the Yule, Reverend
Milo Thornberry of Ellenwood, Georgia, founds Alter-
natives. The nonprofit organization releases a sixteen-
page pamphlet, *Whose Birthday Is It, Anyway?* Catholic
Archdiocese of Detroit buys 12,000 copies, the Evangel-
ical Lutheran Church 19,000.

1975   The pet rock is introduced by an unemployed ad man,
Gary Dahl. Five million pet rocks are sold at $3.95 to $5
each. Extras include owner's manual, gift box with air-
holes, and rock food.[2]

1976   In his Christmas address to a crowd of 100,000 in St.
Peter's Square, Pope Paul says the "emptiness" of modern society has turned youth back to religion and away
from materialism.

1982   Cabbage Patch Kids become the best-selling Christmas
toy of all time (sales figures to 1990: $1.7 billion), later
to be rivaled only by Super Nintendo. (See "Nutcrackers, Ninjas, and Nintendo," page 132.)

1988   On a shopping spree in an L.A. mall with the Secret
Service, President Reagan buys a stuffed Mickey Mouse
and a chocolate Santa for Nancy, plus Disney cartoon
golf balls for himself. (See "Gifts and Stocking Stuffers
of the Rich and Famous," page 111.)

1989   Net American toy profits for the holiday season hit the
$10 billion mark.

---

[2]Dahl dreams up the product at a bar while hearing friends complain about the incon-
veniences of pet ownership. Soon afterward, he collects three tons of pet rock inventory from a Mexican beach.

1989   *Fortune* magazine gives George Plimpton $10,000 to Christmas shop for people who seem to have everything. He buys Norman Mailer a one-man dance band; Florence Joyner a bronze cast of her feet; Ralph Lauren a canine "finishing course" for his sheepdog, Rugby.

1994   According to PNC Bank Corp's Christmas Price Index, the cost of all the gifts in "The Twelve Days of Christmas" reaches an all-time high of $15,944.20. The costliest items: Seven Swans-a-Swimming ($7,000), Nine Ladies Dancing ($2,606.83), and Ten Lords-a-Leaping ($3,012.63).

Dollars and Frankincents

THANK YOU, GOD, FOR CHRISTMAS!

—Holiday sign in a Toyko department store beside a painting
of a Japanese Last Supper. Twelve businessmen swing beer mugs, dance,
and sing karaoke songs. Christ benevolently looks on.

As no one needs to be reminded, Christmas present is a bit more costly than Christmas past. Americans spent $55 billion for gifts in 1994, up from $37 billion in 1987. The Japanese laid out $7.5 billion during the 1993 Christmas season, up from $5.23 billion in 1990.

According to the Gallup poll, the average American currently spends $734 on gifts,[3] and 97 percent of the population buys presents. But does this almost unanimous participation in holiday shopping indicate that the pastime is popular?

[3]And 24 percent of the survey group said they spend $1 to $300; 30 percent spend $301 to $600; 20 percent, $601 to $1,000; 14 percent, $1,001 or more; and 1 percent spend nothing. The holidays generate 19 percent of annual retail spending in the U.S.

Apparently not. The same poll found that only 28 percent of Americans say they "enjoy Christmas shopping a great deal." And 26 percent said it was their "most hated" holiday activity.

Researchers found that men comprised the majority of the 72 percent who said they did not enjoy shopping a great deal.[4] They also found that this lack of enjoyment often led to procrastination: of the 29 percent of the population still shopping on Christmas Eve, most are men. Conversely, the percentage of women who say they start Christmas shopping before Thanksgiving is an impressive 62.

Now a few more telling facts and figures before we head into the mall and do some shopping ourselves:

- Average number of gifts wrapped currently in the typical American household: 29.5.
- Miles of Christmas wrapping paper sold in 1994 by American Greetings: 1.7 billion linear feet (it would circle the earth 12 times).
- Owners who say they give gifts to their pets on Christmas or Hanukkah: 48 percent.[5]
- Percentage of people who say they didn't get what they wanted for Christmas last year: 6.
- Percentage of presents which are returned: 15.
- Percentage of men who return them: 28.
- Percentage of women who don't mind if a gift is returned: 77.[6]
- Percentage of Americans who say they customarily display an unwanted gift: 47.
- Percentage who say they display it only if the giver visits: 24.
- Companies giving employee holiday gifts or bonuses: 35. Percentage of companies which give a turkey or a ham: 39.

---

[4]As a result, mail order is booming. In the last two seasons, more than a quarter of Christmas gifts in America were secured by catalog. Shopping services also now abound from coast to coast. Among them: Born to Shop, Inc.; At Your Beck and Call; EHB Executive Gifts; Lollipop Shopping Service; Mrs. B—Your Personal Shopper.

[5]According to this 1994 *USA Today* poll, 17 percent of pet owners also give presents to their pets on a birthday; 4 percent on Easter; 3 percent on Valentine's Day; and 20 percent when the pet learns a new trick.

[6]According to this 1994 *Redbook* poll, 6 percent of respondents said they would feel "insulted" if a gift was returned; 16 percent wouldn't want to know; and 1 percent didn't know how they'd feel.

- Percentage of a sample group of 2,230 college students who said in 1993 that the perfect gift would be a job from their dream company: 43.
- Percentage of this group who said they would forego all other holiday gifts and celebrations in exchange for a such a job: 53.

Celebrity
Santa Lists

The real meaning of Christmas is what you can do

for others—giving.

—Tipper Gore, *Ladies' Home Journal*, December 1994

Celebrities are among the most generous holiday gift-givers, and the most discriminating receivers. Oprah Winfrey reportedly sends out a forty-five-question gift survey which each member of her staff completes. "Name five really expensive gift items that I would cry with delight if I received," the survey begins.

In the 1992 season, responses from her producers ranged from "a summerhouse in Tuscany" to "a gold Porsche" to "anything by Modigliani" or "a lifetime supply of Prozac."

"Name five things that would make me very happy to receive as a gift," the survey continues. Among the responses here: an Armani overcoat, karaoke laser discs, a tobaggan.

The queen of daytime TV has given her staff members everything from diamond earrings to antique furniture to fully loaded Jeep Cherokees. They, on the other hand, without benefit of a completed questionnaire from their boss—who grossed $98 million in 1993—have been more hard-pressed to find the perfect something for her.

Among the gifts Oprah received from her people in the 1992 season, according to *Redbook* magazine: a set of eight bathing suits ("one for each day"); a framed pair of Lucille Ball's false eyelashes ("with certificate of authenticity"); and—her favorite—a travelogue videotape of a hunt for the perfect Christmas gift for her which ended at her birthplace in Kosciusko, Mississippi, and climaxed with the musical theme "Ain't No Mountain High Enough."

Though the average shopper does not have Oprah Winfrey on his or her list, who among us does not have at least one person who, though they may not be a celebrity exactly, are almost as challenging to shop for?

Last season *The Wall Street Journal* boosted consumer confidence on this question when they asked Home Depot, JCPenney, L. L. Bean, Saks, the Sharper Image, and Tiffany for gift ideas for Newt Gingrich, Colin Powell, and Bill Gates, among other tough shops. Here are some of the suggestions the retailers came up with, chosen from their own inventory, with a $200 price cap:

NEWT GINGRICH

Profile: Speaker of the House of Representatives; American and military history buff; animal lover.

- The Sharper Image: Authentic East German Navy Officer's Coat. Price: $69. "This is a Cold War memento that he can wear," noted Sharper Image gift consultant.
- Tiffany & Co.: Crystal Gavel Paperweight. Price: $175. "For restoring order to the house."
- Saks Fifth Avenue: Handblown Animal Christmas Tree Ornaments—an elephant, zebra, lion, monkey, and giraffe. Price: $18 (each).

COLIN POWELL

Former Chairman of Joint Chiefs of Staff. Possible 1996 presidential candidate. Hobby: vintage Volvo repair.

- Home Depot: A 93-Piece Husky Steel Metric Tool Set. Price: $50.
- JCPenney: Replica of U.S. Capitol Building, a 69-piece, 3-D Puzzle. Price: $34.99.
- L. L. Bean: Petzl Micro Headlamp. High-performance lamp that straps onto the head. Features a spotlight-to-floodlight zoom lens. Price: $27.50.

BILL GATES

Profile: CEO of Microsoft Corp. Computer whiz. Wealthiest man in U.S., worth $9.3 billion. Owns a new mansion and three cars. Newlywed.

- Home Depot: Genie Heavy-Duty Garage-Door Opener. Price: $160.
- Saks Fifth Avenue: Lunch for Two. From New York's Carnegie Deli—via FedEx—consisting of corned beef and pastrami on rye, cream sodas in Saks Fifth Avenue glasses, and cheesecake. Price: $60.
- Tiffany & Co.: Sterling Silver Yo-Yo, engraved with Microsoft Logo. Price: $75, plus engraving cost. "For the child in him."

Gifts and Stocking Stuffers of the Rich and Famous: A Historic Comparison Chart[7]

s we see from the following chart, in some respects holiday giftgiving has changed dramatically over the years, in others it has remained the same — at least among the big spenders.

PRECIOUS & SEMIPRECIOUS ITEMS

FROM	TO	GIFT
Wise Men (4 B.C.)	Jesus	Frankincense, myrrh, gold
King Hussein (1970)	President Nixon	Mother-of-pearl Nativity scene
Bill Clinton (1992)	Hillary	Birthstone (in return Hillary gave Bill golf clubs)

[7]Sources: *Redbook*, *Ladies' Home Journal*, *In Style*, various newspapers, and historical texts.

Madonna (1992)	Melissa, her assistant	Cartier watch (packed in a box of bubblegum)
Jack Gordon (1989), LaToya Jackson's husband-to-be	LaToya Jackson	Five-carat diamond ring (Said Jackson of the Christmas engagement ring: "At first, I didn't want it; he was my manager. I felt it was on the personal side. I was shocked. But I ended up taking it anyway. It's kind of hard to say no to a diamond.")
Danny DeVito (1992)	His staff	Cash

COLLECTIBLES, KNICK-KNACKS, & HOUSES

FROM	TO	GIFT
Naina Yeltsin (1991)	Barbara Bush	Brass vase with filigree flower pattern
Gustavo Diaz Ordaz, President of Mexico (1965)	President Johnson	Sterling-silver vermeil powder box, with gold-and-silver pumpkin design
Liz Taylor (1992)	Jose Eber, her hairdresser	Pratesi sheets ($1,000 per set)
Barbra Streisand (1992)	Her hair-colorist	A Tiffany memo pad, and framed photo of herself
Shabba Ranks, Reggae singer (hits: "House Call," "Slow and Sexy") (1994)	His mom	A $1 million house (with bedroom for himself, with ceiling mirror)

APPAREL & ACCESSORIES

FROM	TO	GIFT
Captain Meriwether Lewis (1805)	Captain William Clark	"Fleece hosiery, shirt, drawers, and socks" (according to Lewis & Clark's expedition journal)
Quentin Tarantino, Movie director (*Reservoir Dogs*, *Pulp Fiction*, etc.) (1993)	Friends and relatives	Socks
President Andrew Jackson's niece (1835)	President Jackson	Slippers (plus: corncob pipe and tobacco bag)
Nancy Reagan (1985)	President Reagan	A sport jacket
Scarlett O'Hara, Heroine, *Gone With the Wind* (1865)	Ashley Wilkes	A homemade sash
Angelica Huston (1992)	Tommy Baratta, her chef	Silk scarf, monogrammed (name misspelled)
Ted Turner (1992)	His CNN reporters	Navy-and-white throw blankets emblazoned with network logo
Queensboro Bridge Celebration Committee (1908)	Queens Tugboat captains	Christmas stockings with sou'wester hats and photos of girls willing to marry seamen. (The stockings were hung low on bridge girders so passing tugboat men could snag them with boat hooks)

PETS

FROM	TO	GIFT
St. Louis, King of France (1236)	Henry III, King of England	A live elephant (In spite of the gift, four years later Henry—known for pugnacity—invaded France.)
President Reagan (1985)	Nancy	Rex, a King Charles Spaniel
Governor Mario Cuomo (1994)	Ms. Broughton, his assistant	His three-year-old German shepherd, Cara (Unseated from office, Cuomo was moving to Manhattan and felt Cara would prefer to stay in Albany.)
Roxy, Sonny, Nugget, and Casey (dogs of Steve Lawrence and Eydie Gorme) (1990)	Bob Newhart's and Perry Como's dogs; Frank Sinatra's parrot	Christmas pillows, charms, and/or dishes

BODY PARTS OR SURGICAL PROCEDURES

FROM	TO	GIFT
Van Gogh (1888)	Rachel, a French prostitute	His right ear (The artist delivered the gift to Rachel on Christmas Eve, wrapped in his hankie.)
Joan Rivers (1993)	Her producers	Holiday plastic surgery procedure of choice

Biggest, Best, & Worst

BIGGEST CHRISTMAS GIFT

A prefab twenty-two-room mansion ordered in 1892 by Jeremiah Nunan, the richest man in Jacksonville, Oregon, for his wife, Delia. The mansion appeared in a catalog from a Tennessee construction firm. House parts were shipped to Delia in fourteen boxcars. Shipment included drapes, carpets, gaslights, wallpaper, plumbing, and a construction foreman, "Big Mick."

MOST EXPENSIVE ADULT CHRISTMAS GIFT

A sixty-five-foot personal luxury submarine, *The Nomad 1000,* offered in the holiday catalog of U.S. Submarines, Anacortes, Washington. *The Nomad* featured two 250-horse diesel engines, and was submersible for up to ten days at 1,000 feet. Its amenities included: plush seats, walnut tables, hot shower, and toilet with—according to

U.S. Subs president Bruce Jones—"an incredible view." Price: $30 million (six-week training course included).

MOST EXPENSIVE KIDDIE CHRISTMAS GIFT (AGE 2–4)

"My First 'Vette": a limited-edition FAO Schwarz miniature '57 Corvette: four feet long, pedal-powered, and "crafted with exquisite detail." Price: $4,500 (adjustable rearview mirrors included).

GREATEST CHRISTMAS GIFT SCAM

In the 1983 season, during the height of "Cabbage Patch Madness," a Milwaukee radio station announced that two-thousand dolls would be air-dropped from a B-29 over County Stadium. Parents were instructed to bring catcher's mitts and credit cards to be aerial-photoed. Two dozen showed up in frigid December weather and waited excitedly for raining Cabbage Patch Kids. And waited. And waited . . .

BEST CHRISTMAS GIFT: 1987

(ACCORDING TO ALTERNATIVES, INC., THE NONPROFIT "KICK THE COMMERCIAL CHRISTMAS HABIT" ORGANIZATION)

A traveling salesman from Sharon, Massachusetts, promised, when home, to spend one hour a day with his son "to do anything you want."

WORST CHRISTMAS GIFT: 1987

(ACCORDING TO ALTERNATIVES, INC.)

A comb-and-brush set given to a New Jersey cancer patient who had gone bald from chemotherapy.

THREE BEST-SELLING CHRISTMAS GIFTS
AT THE NIXON LIBRARY: 1994

- The Nixon and Elvis T-shirt with "Dream Team" insignia commemorating the day in 1970 when the president shook hands with the King in the Oval Office. Price: $18.50.
- The Nixon Yorba Linda Birthplace Birdhouse: $45. (According to the Library Catalog, this item is: "Redesigned as presidential quarters for your fine feathered friends.")
- Rose-scented potpourri made from wreaths for Nixon's funeral: $20.

Five Best-Selling
Christmas Gifts: 1994
· · · · · · · · · · · · · ·

· Mighty Morphin Power Ranger Action Figures

· Kenny G's *Miracles: The Holiday Album*

· The SnakeLight by Black & Decker

· The Wonderbra

· *Crossing the Threshold of Hope,*
by His Holiness John Paul II

Neiman's Noel:
A Retrospective
Catalog

Neiman Marcus has long been the home of some of the most unique seasonal "Supergifts" available. Though not suited for every pocketbook, the holiday catalog of the Dallas department store has always been an interesting browse, especially for adventurous couples. Here are some of Neiman's most romantic offerings from the last three decades:

1963   Submarine built for two: $18,700.

1967   His and Her Camels: $4,125.

1968   His and Her Jaguars. His XKE: $5,559. Her coat: $5,975.

1970   Modern Noah's Ark, built to exact original specs (except unobtainable gopherwood): $588,247.

1971   Two-thousand-year-old His and Her Mummy Cases: $16,000.

1978   His and Her Natural Safety Deposit Boxes: twin Colorado caves fitted out as safe deposit vaults: $90,000.

1979   His and Her hot-air balloons: $50,000.

1981   His and Her Robot: $15,000.

1991   His and Her Hummer, all-terrain, diesel-powered vehicles
        (used in Operation Desert Storm, and popularized for pri-
        vate use by Arnold Schwarzenegger): $50,000.
        Limited-edition hoof-signed painting by Ruby, an
        eighteen-year-old abstract-expressionist elephant at
        Phoenix Zoo: $40.
1993   Life-size, computerized triceratops dinosaur: $93,000.[8]

---

[8]The last item was purchased by a Middle Eastern ambassador in Washington. The
dinosaur was shipped to Aspen, where it became the centerpiece for a New Year's Eve
party.

Just Say Noel
Gift List:
An Official
Catalog for Men
Who Hate the
Yule, and
Women Who
Have to Shop
for Them

I n his 1993 article for *The American Economic Review,* Yale professor Joel Waldfogel coined an important Noelogism: "Deadweight
Loss." Waldfogel defined DL as: "The difference between what
the gift-giver spent for an item and the value the recipient places on
it."

DL CALCULATION:
Bob receives a glow-in-the-dark necktie from his ex-wife:
she paid $30, he feels it is worth $3.

   DL base: $27 ($30 - $3 = $27)
   DL quotient: 90% ($27 ÷ $30 = 90%)

  In his study of Christmas gift-giving, Waldfogel found that the
current national annual DL base stands at $4 billion; the DL quotient
10 percent.

As we have already seen, judging from their rate of gift return (28 percent), men particularly seem to suffer from Deadweight Loss at Christmastime. No wonder December 26 is both National Whiner's Day and Official God-Awful-Tie Day.

So how does the well-intending woman elude the Scylla and Charybdis of Deadweight Loss when shopping for the special man on her list? Some suggestions of affordable products from season's past, many still available:

$15.50 AND UNDER

THE BEEP SEAT. "An electronic toilet seat reminder." Invented and marketed by San Francisco bank teller Jim Novack, this is a miniature battery-driven alarm which fits on the bottom of a toilet seat and beeps if the seat is not lowered within sixty seconds of being raised. Says Novack, who expected a rush on the product for the 1993 holidays, "I get letters from women—ecstatic women." Beep Seat is available at select California hardware stores, bath shops, and one wine accessory shop in Sonoma. $5.95.

THE RUBBER NECKTIE. Made from whitewall tires by One Song Enterprises, of Willoughby, Ohio, this seasonal favorite for dads carries a full 500-year warranty. $15.50.

AUTHENTIC CORONER'S TOE-TAG KEY CHAIN from L.A. County Coroner's "Skeletons in the Closet" Giftshop. $5.

IRS CHRISTMAS TREE ORNAMENT from the Treasury Historical Association, Washington, D.C. A gold-plated 1913 IRS form commemorating the eightieth anniversary of the agency, it bears the insignia: *Eighty Years of Income Tax. Many Happy Returns.* Proceeds from the ornament are used to help restore the Old Treasury Building in Washington. $11.

ATLANTIS BEACHFRONT. A scroll deed to the lost island, plus a subscription to the Atlantis newsletter, *Life at the Bottom,* available from a Santa Monica company for $14.95.

$39.95 AND UNDER

STARCLONE, a 2-ounce bottle of cologne made from the sweat of Sammy Kershaw, country singer. Special holiday price: $19.95.

POWDERED URINE, guaranteed drug-free, from Byrd Labs of Austin, Texas, "Purveyors of fine urine products." Perfect for the job applicant. $19.95.

THE SULLY NOSE SPREADER from Robert "Sully" Sullivan of Eugene, Oregon. According to the retired engineer's press release, the Spreader prevents occlusion of the nasal passages during sleep, is made of chrome steel, and is "medically safe." Directions for use: "Just before you go to bed, insert it into your nose. Go to bed, and go to sleep, there is no feeling after you insert the spreader in your nose." $18.

THE BOBBITT T-SHIRT. This item was sold in Pittsburgh during the 1993 holiday season to cover the $200,000 of legal fees incurred by John Wayne Bobbitt, the Virginia man whose penis was cut off by his wife, discarded on the greenbelt, and later reattached by surgeons. On the front of the T-shirt was a woman with a fillet knife; on the back the inscription Love Hurts. $25.[9]

ORVIS CRACKER THROWER. According to the catalog, the device can propel a cracker "up to 60 yards at incredible speeds," and is designed to "launch crackers into the air as challenging, biodegradable targets

---

[9]Days before Christmas, USA Today reported that Bobbitt would reveal his reattached organ on a pay-per-view basis during a New Year's Eve cable TV special hosted by New York shock-jock Howard Stern, one of Bobbitt's fund-raisers. When the night came, though he was grossing more than $11 million for his two-hour holiday special (270,000 U.S. households at $40 apiece), Stern lowballed Bobbitt with an indecent $2,000 cash proposal, which he later upped to $15,000, for his guest to "Show the world your scar and everything." Though Bobbitt, according to The Daily News, said he "just couldn't," he joined Joe Frazier and Mark "Skywalker" Hamill to judge forty bikini-clad contestants in the Miss Howard Stern Beauty Pageant. Later, after a year's consideration of Stern's original proposal, Mr. Bobbitt released an adult video for the 1994 holiday season: John Wayne Bobbitt Uncut. The video, which featured the fully operational star au naturale with six women, sold briskly at $59.95.

for trap shooters." It can also be used "at the beach as a seagull feeder." Available in both right-handed and left-handed models at $19.50.

HEIDI FLEISS PLAID CHRISTMAS BOXERS. Sales of men's underwear were brisk during the 1994 season. Tapping the trend, the Hollywood Madam to the Stars, after her conviction on three counts of pandering in December, sold out a large inventory at her "KLSC Classic Rock Expo" booth in L.A. The briefs came with Fleiss's John Hancock and were priced on blow-out at: $24.99.

GRANDMA KEENAN'S FLAMING FRUITCAKE. A compressed sawdust log wrapped like a fruitcake. Six pack: $39.95.[10]

$896 AND UNDER

CHRISTMAS CART DANCE. Gift certificate for golf, dinner, beer, and a "cart dance" by a topless female caddie at Fort Worth's New Orleans Nightclub. $620.

SEVEN-DAY "ALL-NUDE" CHRISTMAS CRUISE. Destination: Caribbean. Carrier: Bare Necessities of Austin, Texas. $896.

$6,500 AND UNDER

MALE PECTORAL IMPLANTS, from Dr. Brian Novack of Beverly Hills. Gift certificate for $6,500.

---

[10]A percentage of proceeds goes to the Leukemia Society of America.

Ditching It Discreetly: A How-to from Miss Manners

L et nothing to dismay, in the 1993 season the maven of good taste gave a step-by-step on how anybody can unload a Deadweight Loser without breaching the laws of etiquette.

- Do some discreet detective work to find out where it comes from and exchange it for something else.
- Donate it to a worthy charity.[11]
- Give it to someone who might like it.
- Throw it into a yard sale.
- Never let the giver know that you didn't like it. Not only does this mean expressing thanks[12] and not inquiring where

[11]In the 1993 season, the QCI Phone Company of New York offered the *Thanks But No Thanks* Christmas gift-return program. Donors of the top 100 rejects received $25 worth of free long-distance phone calls from QCI. All donations went to homeless shelters and Toys for Tots.

[12]Miss Manners suggests the technique for this elsewhere: "The difficulty of conveying the appearance of gratitude is a powerful argument in favor of thank-you letters, as they do not strain the facial muscles."

to return it, but it means choosing a charity, recipient, or yard sale that the original donor will never know about.

This requires some thought. But then, as Miss Manners pointed out, it *is* the thought that counts.[13]

[13]From Miss Manners' 12-19-93 column, "Hate Your Christmas Presents? There are nice ways to handle it."

Chatterbox:
The Thought That Counts

· · · · · · · · · · · · · ·

The ideal Christmas present is money.

The only trouble is, you can't charge it.

—Bill Vaughan

There are generally two kinds of Christmas presents:

the ones you don't like and the ones you don't get.

—Anonymous

What I like about Christmas is that you can make

people forget the past with the present.

—Don Marquis

Two weeks before Christmas, I always think of

a good present for someone but it has to be ordered

three weeks in advance.

—Andy Rooney

A woman never knows what to give her husband for

Christmas until she learns how much he wants to spend.

—Anonymous

It is better to give than to receive a Christmas gift

because you don't have the bother of exchanging it.

—Anonymous

The only gift is a portion of thyself.

Thou must bleed for me!

—Ralph Waldo Emerson

You think she'll like this better than

a diamond bracelet?

—Ronald Reagan, after buying a box of chocolates for his wife
at L.A.'s Century City Shopping Center in 1988

Never give below your taste level.

Never say: "Well, I think it's disgusting, but it's

just the sort of thing she would like."

—Miss Manners

The Price
I$ Right

As every holiday shopper well knows, it does not pay to be haypenny wise and partridge foolish when venturing out into the mall. A working knowledge of comparative prices for seasonal staples is important—not only current prices, but values from Christmases past. Test your holiday shopping I.Q.

1. The current retail cost of a partridge in a pear tree (not including the pear tree) is:
    a. $3.40.
    b. $34.00.
    c. $340.00.
    The current labor cost of eight maids-a-milking (for one hour or less) is:
    a. $3.40.
    b. $34.00.
    c. $340.00.

2. The sale of frankincense boomed in 1993 due to the fall of Marxist oppression and the revival of Catholic churches in the Sultanate of Oman, which sold a record twenty tons of the aro-

matic resin last year. The current street price in Oman for a kilo (2.2 pounds) of frankincense is $560. True or false?

3. The Lionel "Blue Comet" Train, the most popular Christmas toy of the 1920s, went for ———. At collector's auctions, the train now goes for ———.

4. The Hula Hoop, called the "biggest fad in history" and "the granddaddy of American zaniness," sold for $1.98 in the summer of 1958. More than 25 million hoops were sold in four months. But by Christmas, the craze was fading and the price of a Hula Hoop was marked down to:
   a. 99 cents.
   b. 79 cents.
   c. 50 cents.

5. Super Nintendo's Shaqu-Fu, the 1994 season's hottest video game, which shows Shaquille O'Neal of the Orlando Magic battling ninja warriors, sets you back ———.

6. A bag of chocolate-covered Christmas potato chips from Streftel's Candy Factory, Hollywood's premiere confectioner (which supplied edible wedding announcements from Michael Jackson and Lisa Marie Presley), costs: ———.

7. J-B Pet Supplies, in Oakland, New Jersey, sells holiday Reindog antlers for ———, and Reincat antlers for ———.

8. One of the more unique novelty gift items from Hollywood several seasons ago was Celebrity Dirt. Vials of dirt from the lawns and gardens of Liz Taylor, Michael J. Fox, Joan Collins, Katharine Hepburn, and forty-two other celebrities went for the bargain price of:
   a. $2 per dirt vial.
   b. $4.50.
   c. $9.95.[14]

9. A historic gift offering from the 1989 season was The Valdez Vial, which contained an ounce of crude from the 11-million-gallon Exxon spill in Alaska's Prince William Sound. It cost $9.95. True or false?

---

[14]Inventory was personally collected by Celebrity Dirt, Inc., CEO Barry Gibson, using a shovel, plastic trash bag, and Hollywood celebrity map. (In the off-season Gibson ran a janitorial service in Lansing, Michigan.)

10. The cost of a holiday subscription to *The Tightwad Gazette* is:
———.

EXTRA CREDIT
- The cost of a holiday subscription to *The Skinflint News* is:
———.

ANSWER KEY:
1. b. $34.00 (according to PNC Bank Corp's 1994 Christmas Price Index).
b. $34.00.
2. False. The price is $5.60.
3. $10; $8,000.
4. c. 50 cents.
5. $65.
6. $12.50.
7. Reindog antlers, $4.50; Reincat antlers, $3.80.
8. a. $2 per dirt vial.
9. True.
10. $12.

Extra Credit:
- $9.95.

Nutcrackers,
Ninjas,
and Nintendo

In 1843 Tiny Tim didn't ask his father, Bob Cratchit, for anything for Christmas. A century later, in 1946, all Zuzu wanted from Jimmy Stewart in *It's a Wonderful Life* was the petals to be put back on her rose. The next year, 1947, Natalie Wood asked Edmund Gwenn for a house in *Miracle on 34th Street*.

Even the casual observer sees an unsettling seasonal pattern beginning to develop here.

In 1993 *USA Today* polled eight- to eighteen-year-olds on what gifts they most wanted. These were the results: video games: 91 percent; CD players: 58 percent; personal computers: 56 percent; designer jeans: 46 percent.

During the same period *The Wall Street Journal* surveyed several million youngsters ages six to thirteen, asking them what name-brands they most wanted. The top replies: Rollerblades, Sega games, Sony CD players, Timberland boots, and anything worn by the cast of *Beverly Hills, 90210*.

Toys and video games have become holiday blue-chip items. They gross $19 billion annually in the U.S., and Christmas sales account for about 60 percent of the take.

Toys became big business in the 1950s and 1960s with Erector sets, Lionel and HO trains, and Tonka trucks for boys; Betsy Wetsy, Chatty Cathy, Barbie, Shirley Temple, and Tiny Tears dolls for girls. The market continued to expand in the 1970s and 1980s with Cabbage Patch Kids, Ghostbusters, Simpsons, Smurfs, Big Birds, Deely Boppers, and Teenage Mutant Ninja Turtles. Now receipts have gone over the eleven-figure mark with Nintendo, Barneys, Baby Burpys, Magic Marvins, Magic Mikes, and Mighty Morphin Power Rangers.

Three French Hens, Two Turtledoves, and an Incredible Crash Dummy in a Pear Tree

The days of Lincoln Logs, Patty Playpals, and Teddy Ruxpin seem to be long behind us. Here is a minicatalog of some of the best-selling hard-core holiday toys of the last few years.

THE TALKING STIMPY DOLL

(INTERACTIVE TOY "FOR AGES 4 AND UP")
Yank the hair ball in his throat and Stimpy talks. Squeeze his leg and he makes "rude underleg noises."[15]

TONY THE TATTOOED MAN

Box contains Tony and a tattoo gun. Sold separately, a selection of temporary tattoos: "brains, boogers, bugged-out eyes and other anatomical atrocities."

[15]Stimpy's main competitor is "Gak," which also emits rude noises, but looks like slime.

EAT AT RALPH'S

(AGES 5 AND UP)

A 3-D board game with Ralph the fry cook's mouth open in the middle. The object of the game is to stuff Ralph's mouth with pizza, burgers, fries, and soda until he ralphs.

SEGA GENESIS' NIGHT TRAP

Video game in which the player tries to rescue a group of scantily clad girls from a gang of vampires. If the player fails, the vampires draw the girls' blood with neck drills.[16]

TYCO'S INCREDIBLE
CRASH DUMMIES

Starter kit includes a car with driver's side airbag plus one crash dummy. If the dummy does not wear his seat belt when driving into a wall, he flies through the windshield headfirst, shedding body parts. Available at extra cost are Second Generation Dummies: Slick, Axel, Spare Tire, Skid the Kid, and Hubcap.[17]

---

[16]Due to letters of complaint against the game by Senators Joseph Lieberman and Herb Kohl, Toys "R" Us and Kay Bee Toys removed the Night Trap from the shelves during the 1993 holiday season. But Sega's Mortal Kombat—wherein Ninjas do battle, the victor either decapitating his opponent or ripping his heart out—was kept. This game was launched by a $10 million ad campaign and has netted more than $100 million in Christmas sales. In the 1994 season, Sega Genesis scored another hit with "Maximum Carnage" from their Spiderman Venom series.

[17]The idea for Crash Dummies originated with the National Highway Traffic Safety Administration's 1985 campaign to promote seat-belt use. Later, NHTSA commissioned Tyco to develop dummy toys, but soon dissolved the partnership. After spending $3 million in Crash Dummy development, Tyco unveiled the dolls at the1991 American International Toy Fair in New York. They outsold their competitors and grossed over $50 million.

GRAVEYARD GHOULIES
CREATE-A-CORPSE

(AGES 8 AND UP)

"Make 'n' Play Pak" includes a glow-in-the-dark skeleton with all organs needed to "make ghastly guts: brain, heart, lungs, intestines, stomach, and kidneys." A "real molding oven" for organ-baking is available as an extra. (In the 1994 season, Tyco came out with the similar product: Dr. Dreadful Food and Drink Labs—"ideal for whipping up gross yet edible delicacies like monster brains and bursting eyeballs.")

Home Alone 2–Revisited:
For the Kid Who Has
Everything (Else)

In 1992 the New York Plaza Hotel introduced the *Home Alone 2* package. It allows the youngster an opportunity to relive the most popular Christmas movie of all time. Just $1,100 pays for one night in the "Kevin Suite" (#411), early admission to FAO Schwarz the next morning, plus a room-service "Kevin Sundae"–an M&M banana split with almond slivers and rainbow sprinkles under umbrellas.

The Frankincents Final

I n closing, some multiple-choice, true-false, and fill-in-the-blank questions on basic shopping and gift-giving from Christmases past to present:

1. The names of the original three gift-givers, The Magi, were: Gaspar (meaning "white"), Melchior ("light"), and Balthasar ("the lord of the treasury"). True or false?
2. Besides the prize turkey, what did Scrooge give his clerk Bob Cratchit for Christmas after being visited by the three ghosts?
   a. A day off.
   b. A pen-and-pencil set.
   c. Grandma Keenan's Flaming Fruitcake.
   d. A raise in salary.
   e. Atlantis beachfront.
3. Who wrote this in her Christmas diary: "I gave Mamma a bracelet made of my hair, and the Keepsake, and Oriental Annual. I stayed up til eleven!"
   a. Queen Victoria.
   b. Eleanor Roosevelt.

    c. Chelsea Clinton.

    d. Brooke Shields.

4. "Hello, Boys! Make Lots of Toys!" This was the famous holiday advertising slogan for what best-selling toy of 1913?

5. "He Put Tracks Beneath the Christmas Tree." This was the title of a *Reader's Digest* biographical profile of: ————.

6. In 1971 the Women's Equalization Committee of Los Angeles gave men a $1 Christmas gift idea for their wives. It was:

    a. A specially priced holiday issue of *Ladies' Home Journal*.

    b. A gold-leafed draft of the Equal Rights Amendment.

    c. A sample box of All-Temperature Cheer.

    d. A gift certificate guaranteeing wives a 50 percent share in family assets.

7. In 1987 Crown Books reported that its national holiday sales of the Bible were in a dead heat with those of:

    a. The novels of Stephen King.

    b. The novels of Judith Krantz.

    c. *All I Need to Know, I Learned in Kindergarten*.

    d. *How the Grinch Stole Christmas*.

8. Name a few popular adult holiday stress toys from the 1980s and early 1990s.

9. For Christmas 1993, O.J. Simpson gave Nicole ————; Nicole gave O.J. a ————; and O.J. gave Cora Fischman, Nicole's friend and neighbor, a ————.

DOUBLE JEOPARDY

10. For Christmas 1994, Robert Shapiro, defense attorney in O.J.'s murder trial, gave to select reporters:

    a. Pen-and-pencil sets.

    b. Bijan's "DNA" perfume.

    c. Heidi Fleiss boxers.

    d. Kenny G's *Miracles: The Holiday Album*.

    e. Pope John Paul's *Crossing the Threshhold of Hope*.

EXTRA CREDIT

- As an alternative to GI Joe, Mighty Morphin Power Ranger, and Masters of the Universe, Christian toy companies Wee Win, Rainfall, and Praise Unlimited offer:

a. "Biblical action figures" Jesus, Samson, David, and Goliath.
b. "Kingdom Critters."
c. "Prince of Peace Pets."
d. "Grace, the Pro-Life Doll."
e. All of the above.

ANSWER KEY:
1. True.
2. d. A raise in salary.
3. d. Queen Victoria, at age seventeen, in 1836. She also listed some of the Christmas gifts she received from "good Louis, Uncle Leopold, the Queen, and dear Mamma." These included: "a lovely button with an angel's head," "a lovely coloured sketch of dearest Aunt Louise," "a beautiful piece of Persian snuff," and "two almanacks."
4. Erector set.
5. Joshua Lionel Cowen, inventor of Lionel trains.
6. d. $1 gift certificate guaranteeing wives a 50 percent share in family assets.
7. b. The novels of Judith Krantz.
8. • Rx Freud Stress Bouncer: A rubber ball that let out an electronic scream when paddled.
   • Woes B. Gone: A wind-up doll that "does your pacing for you."
   • Sammy-Slam-Me doll: When punched, Sammy drove a peg up a carnival stress meter topped with a bell.
   • Bloomingdale's O-No Worry Talking Pillow ($25) which said: "Oh, worry, worry, worry!. Money! My boss! My mother-in-law! Oh, no. The tax man! Bills. Bills. Bills! Oh, no. The stock market! Oh, worry, worry, worry!"
9. Six-carat diamond drop earrings; gift certificate for private training sessions at an L.A. gym; Swiss Army knife.

Double Jeopardy:
10. b. Bijan's "DNA" perfume.

Extra Credit:
   • e. All of the above.

V.

The Goose Is Getting Fat

Holiday Food and Drink

… A great goose, applesauce, mashed potatoes …

and a pudding blazing in a pint of fiery brandy.

—Charles Dickens, *A Christmas Carol,*
of the spread at the Cratchit household, 1843

Hot chocolate. With whipped cream on top.

Really hot …. Dreidels … Potato latkes … Roasted

chestnuts~yes, on an open fire. You bought them

by the bag. God, they were delicious! I don't know why,

but they tasted better then than now.

—Larry King, 1993, on his favorite holiday treats as a boy in Brooklyn

A Brief History of Toms, Dickens, and Jerry

Our holiday dinner has its roots in pagan fertility feasts. Even so, some of the hardiest old-time holiday diners were friars popularly known as the Merry Monks. One merry group, the brothers of St. Swithin at Winchester, made an official complaint to King Henry II when their abbot attempted to cut three dishes from their customary thirteen-course Christmas menu.

Medieval royalty was as keen on holiday fare as was the clergy. When, in 1252, King Henry III threw a potluck supper celebrating both the Yule and the marriage of his daughter, Margaret, to Alexander, King of Scots, he supplied two tons of white wine and one of red, while the archbishop of York provided six hundred oxen, drawn and quartered. A century later, King Richard II invited ten thousand guests to a holiday gala at the newly remodeled Westminster Hall, and there the celebrants consumed twenty-eight oxen, three hundred sheep, and two thousand fowl.

The royal Christmas banquets of the Middle Ages traditionally started at three in the afternoon, lasted till twelve, and included fortified mulled wines and at least ten main courses preceded by exotic appetizers. In 1415 King Henry V began his Christmas feast with

"Dates in composite, carp, turbot and tench in mottled cream, sturgeon with whelks, fried mimis, and roast porpoise garnished with figures of angels." Following these hors d'oeuvres, a seventeen-course dinner was served, then dessert. Finally, just before midnight, a tub of steaming punch with oysters and pheasants was wheeled in as a "palate cleanser."

How did we get from this point to our Butterballs, turnips, and Del Monte cranberry mold today? Our next Nut & Dateline provides some of the culinary milestones.

563   The cardinals at the Council of Braga forbid fasting on Christmas Day.

1520   The Prince of Borghese orders in a six-meter-long Magi Cake frosted with his coat of arms.

1580   Sir William Petrie throws the largest Christmas feed for commoners: 17 oxen are consumed. Plus: 14 steers, 5 bacon hogs, 13 bucks, 29 calves, 54 lambs, 129 sheep. And 1 ton of cheese. (For other culinary records, see "Astronomic Gastronomic," page 161.)

1786   George Washington, away from Mount Vernon over the holidays, writes to a friend saying he sorely misses his wife, Martha's, annual "attack of Christmas pies." (For Martha's Yorkshire pie recipe see "Historic Holiday Menus and Recipes," page 153.)

1800   Koba hunters develop the first native African Christmas menu: Entrée: *Points d'éléphant* (elephant trunk and feet); Dessert: Plum pudding *Sans Réproche*.

1826   "The Eggnog Riot" breaks out at West Point Military Academy after superintendent Sylvanus Thayer decrees the first dry Yule: 70 cadets consume vats of nog and riot, 19 are court-martialed, 11 dismissed, 6 resign.

1843   The Ghost of Christmas Present appears in Scrooge's dining room mounted on "a throne of turkeys, great joints of meat, and fruits of every description."

1890   The Tom and Jerry drink is developed.

1930   *Niños Envueltos* or "wrapped children" (stuffed steaks) become the favorite dish in Argentina.

1965   The pope lets individual bishops decide whether Catholics may eat meat on Christmas Eve, which falls on a Friday that year. Cardinal Spellman frees New Yorkers of the obligation to abstain.

1990   Kentucky Fried Chicken of Japan introduces the $29 "Christmas Barrel" as an alternative to turkey. On Christmas Eve Japanese KFC outlets move $14.7 million worth of Christmas Barrels (five times the quantity of chicken they sell on the average day).

1990   The U.S. Army puts together a ten-million-pound Christmas menu for 300,000 Desert Shield servicemen in Saudi Arabia.

1990   The U.S. Department of Agriculture reports that Americans consume 22 million turkeys and 102 million cans of cranberry at Christmastime. The U.S. Council of Distilled Spirits reports consumption of 98 million quarts of eggnog and 81 million gallons of liquor.

1993   Americans consume 6 percent more turkeys, cans of cranberry, quarts of nog, etc., than in 1990. Weight Watchers kicks off an aggressive national Lose 10 Pounds America Challenge Program.

1994   President and Mrs. Clinton throw a Christmas feast for two thousand reporters at the White House. The menu includes: caviar, pickled shrimp, baby lamb chops, seared chicken with dried fruit, roast goose stuffed with bread and apples, passion fruit mousse, and truffles spiked with Jack Daniel's. Drinks include Chivas Regal and "secret-recipe" eggnog.

Food & Drink[1]

- Number of turkeys consumed in the U.S. between Thanksgiving and Christmas, 1994: 97 million.
- Gallons of gravy consumed: 21 million.
- Amount spent on liquor, December 1994. $8.9 million.
- Pounds of fruitcake sold by America's leading fruitcake manufacturer, Claxton Fruitcakes, Georgia, 1994: 4.5 million (up from 17,000 in 1954).
- Percentage of Americans who say they ate plum pudding last Christmas: 1 percent.
- Percentage of Americans who ate Christmas dinner at home in 1992: 46.
  Percentage who ate with parents or in-laws: 29.
  With their grown-up children: 8.
  With some other relative: 10.
  With friends: 5.
  At a restaurant: 1.
  Alone: 2.
- Pounds of See's Candies sold at 215 retail stores and by mail during the 1987 holiday season: 12 million.
- Percentage of Americans who in 1985 said they found normal-weight people "a lot more attractive" than heavier-set people: 55.
- Percentage of Americans who in 1994 said they found normal-weight people "a lot more attractive" than heavier-set people: 32.

[1]Sources: USA Today, The New York Times, The Wall Street Journal, Harper's Index, 1987–94.

Of Birds, Boar, and Barons of Beef: Facts about Old-Fashioned Christmas Fare

OF BIRDS

The staple of holiday dinners in Europe and America until the nineteenth century was mincemeat pie with the works. As an old saying in England went, "The Devil himself dare not appear in Cornwall during Christmas for fear of being baked in a pie." A noted churchman once said, "Such pye is an hodge-podge of superstition, Popery, the devil, and all its works. It is an idolatrie in crust!" A common ingredient of the pies was fowl of every sort, the more exotic the better.

In 1171 King Henry II held a Christmas feast for all the dignitaries of Ireland, who, reported a royal chronicler, "were with difficulty prevailed on by His Majestie to eat the flesh of cranes."

The largest Christmas bird pie of all time was Sir Henry Grey's legendary 9-foot diameter, 165-pounder in 1770. It contained: 2 bushels of flour, 20 pounds of butter, 7 blackbirds, 6 pigeons, 6 snipes, 4 geese, 4 partridges, 4 wild ducks, 2 woodcocks, 2 curlews, 2 rabbits, and 2 neat's tongues.

The peacock in a medieval Christmas pie was often arranged so that its head protruded from one side of the crust, its tail plumage from the other. The beak was gilded, a sponge was saturated with spirits and placed inside it, then lighted as the bird was served. On occasion the bird was not lighted because it was still alive.[2]

The medieval form of today's New Year's Resolution was called the Knight's Peacock Vow. At the last feast of Christmas week, the knight would place his right hand on the back of the bird and make a solemn pledge (such as to defend the virtue of ladies, to fight the infidel, etc.).

Christmas pies were often stolen and had to be carefully protected. Wrote the poet Robert Herrick in the seventeenth century:

> *Come guard the Christmas pie*
> *That the thief, though ne'er so shy,*
> *With his flesh-hooks don't come nigh,*
> *To catch it.*

King Henry VIII's favorite holiday bird dish was Peacock Enkakyll. Here is the seven-step recipe taken from the Royal Cookbook of 1497:

Step 1: Take a peacock, break its neck, and cut its throat.

Step 2: Flay off the skin with the feathers, tail, and the neck and head thereon.

Step 3: Take the skin with all the feathers, lay it on the table abroad, and strew thereon ground cinnamon.

Step 4: Roast the peacock, and baste him with raw yolks of eggs.

Step 5: When he is roasted, take him off, and let him cool awhile.

Step 6: Gild his comb, then wind his skin, feathers, and tail about his body.

Step 7: Serve him forth as he were alive.

---

[2]According to Phillipa Pullar in her book *Consuming Passions*: "At many feasts, birds, mammals and reptiles flew, wriggled and hopped from the dishes for the astonishment of the guests. After a while birds and frogs were considered dull stuff . . . Toy terriers, hares, foxes, and dwarfs all emerged at one time or another."

OF BOAR

Boar was served from the earliest holidays, mouth stuffed. An old legend explains how this tradition got started:

One winter's day, a young student was reading Aristotle in Shotover Forest when suddenly he was charged by a wild boar. He rammed his Aristotle into the boar's jaws and, "choking the savage with the sage," exclaimed, *"Graecum est!"* ("Greece lives!") The young man brought the boar's head back home triumphantly and there retrieved his copy of Aristotle from its jaws. And ever since that day, a boar's head has been carried to the Christmas table with the words:

> *Quot estis in convivio.*
> *Caput apri defero*
> *Reddens laudes Domino!"*
> [*The boar's head in hand bear I,*
> *Bedeck'd with bays and rosemary:*
> *And I pray you, my masters, be merry!*]

OF BARONS OF BEEF

Ox beef was the other popular Old World holiday entrée, particularly the loin cuts. These were given honorary titles by King Charles II himself. One Christmas the monarch sat down to a very large feast and, after draining several aperitifs, suddenly drew his sword, laid it on the entrée, and made this historic declaration to his lords:

Gentleman! Fond as I am of all of you, yet I have a still greater favorite—the loin of a good beef. Therefore, good beef roast, I knight thee Sir Loin, and I proclaim that a double loin be known as a Baron!

Turkey
Trivia

The conquistadors brought New World turkeys to Europe in the early 1500s. Providing a welcome holiday alternative to the comparatively petite pigeon, peacock, and guinea hen, the succulent gobblers soon gained popularity with kings and commoners alike.

But it took American energy and ingenuity to make the turkey big business. Here are some marketing milestones in the career of the holiday bird that Ben Franklin recommended to be our national emblem, in preference to the eagle, which he called "a robber, a sharper, and a bird of bad moral character."

THE MONSTER TURKEY

American turkey farms flourished from Connecticut to Ohio by the mid-1800s. Top producers soon began to compete to see who could grow the biggest gobbler. In 1860, a record 34-pounder was exhibited in New York. Breed-and-feed experiments in the next decades yielded substantially bigger birds. On Christmas Day in 1893, a record 61-pounder was served at New York's Plaza Hotel. But, the true heavyweight champ was not seen until 1913. His name was Buster, owned by Charles Aumiller of Crawford County, Ohio, and he weighed 80 pounds. Aumiller was trying to put a few more pounds on Buster for Christmas, but the tom expired on the scales six days shy of the Yule. The cause of death, according to the *New York Tribune's* obituary: coronary due to fatty degeneration of the heart.

TURKEY DRIVES

In the Old West, gobblers were driven to market in herds like cattle. And time was of the essence: a fast turkey drive was a profitable turkey drive. The fastest on record occurred in 1863: two turkeyboys drove a flock of five-hundred from Missouri to Denver in twenty-eight days. The flock was fed on range grasshoppers and shelled corn. Another historic turkey drive was led by one Henry C. Hooker during the Gold Rush. With the aid of only a handful of turkeydogs and one turkeyboy, Hooker drove his stock from Hangtown, California, across the High Sierras to Carson City, Nevada. Rich prospectors paid him so much for his Christmas birds ($5 apiece) that Hooker retired from the poultry transport business and started a cattle ranch in Arizona.

CORBIN'S GREAT GOBBLER GIVEAWAY

Well before the turn of the century, companies began distributing holiday turkeys to employees. One of the largest gobbler giveaways occurred in 1883 when Austin Corbin, director of the Long Island Railroad, personally dropped off a frozen bird to each of his 1,200 employees. Corbin's "Turkey Train," decorated with evergreen and holly and a MERRY CHRISTMAS! banner, departed Long Island City station on December 23. Aboard the baggage car were 1,200 frozen turkeys, each bearing a tag with an employee name attached to the left drumstick, plus a letter of Season's Greetings from Mr. Corbin himself. On the 260-mile trip, the tycoon entertained personal holiday guests in his dining car: the group ate, drank champagne, smoked

Havanas, sang, and played poker. When the "Turkey Train" returned to Long Island City, not a single bird was aboard. But there were hundreds of empty champagne bottles and cigar boxes.

QUEEN VIC'S CORN-FED CONNECTICUT TOM

By the end of the nineteenth century, the top turkey-producing state in the Union was Connecticut, followed by Rhode Island and New York. So sought-after had Connecticut gobblers become that Queen Victoria herself ordered one from top producer L. Main of Swanton Hill. Main dispatched to Her Majesty his finest corn-fed, grasshopper-fattened, dry-picked 40-pounder. The price of the royal bird: $13.

"TURKEY POWER"

Exploiting the popularity of poultry, politicians soon began to run on what journalists dubbed "Turkey Power." Near the turn of the century, Congressman "Big Tim" and son "Little Tim" Sullivan of New York gave out thousands of birds to Bowery residents. In 1898 John Powers, the Chicago alderman, broke all records by handing out fourteen tons of turkey and geese to three thousand families. The trend soon reached the White House. In 1907 Teddy Roosevelt distributed the first presidential turkeys. His steward, Henry Pickney, rode to Washington's Centery Market by covered wagon and loaded it up with 125 toms for married White House staff members. To avoid unseasonable squabbling or complaint, the president had staffers draw lots. As a result, William Loeb, his stenographer, got a smaller bird than the man who dusted his desk.

Historic
Holiday Menus
and Recipes

Now, for a *Just Say Noel!* smorgasbord featuring some of the most memorable holiday feeds of the last five centuries—from Westminster Hall to the White House, from the ice caps of Greenland to the African outback:

CHRISTMAS DINNER WITH
QUEEN KATHERINE

(1426)

This feast was held at Westminster Hall. Guests included the archbishop of Canterbury (seated at the queen's right), the king of Scotland (at her left), and other VIPs. Sir Richard Nevill carved. The earl of Suffolk bore cups. Lord Audley passed the almonds. And the earl of Worchester rode about the hall during dinner on his charger, keeping order. The dinner included thirteen courses. Here are the first two, plus cocktails:

APPETIZER

"Brawn and mustard, dedells in burneauz, frument with balien, pike in herbs, powdered lamprey, and eels roasted with lamprey." This, plus a "Subtletie" (a sugar sculpture) of "a pelican sitting on her nest with young, and St. Katherine holding a book and disputing with the doctors."

FIRST COURSE

"Jelly coloured with columbine flowers, white potage, bream of the sea, conger, soles, cheven, barbel with roach, and fresh salmon." (Plus another sugar sculpture of a panther and St. Katherine.)

COCKTAILS

"Pigment, morat, mead, hypocras (wine mixed with honey), claret (clarified wine with spices), cider, perry, and ale."

CHRISTMAS DINNER WITH
GEORGE AND MARTHA WASHINGTON

(MOUNT VERNON—1797)

Busy with affairs of war and state, our first president missed many holiday dinners at home. But on retirement in 1797 he made up for this. His favorite fare was said to be Martha's Yorkshire pie and her "Forty Youlk Frensh Brandy Cake." Here is the recipe for the Yorkshire pie:

Step 1: Boil: 1 turkey, 1 goose, 1 partridge, 1 pigeon, 1 hare, 3 woodcocks, and 3 moorhens.

Step 2: Mix together: ½ ounce of mace, of nutmeg, of cloves, of white pepper, and 2 heaping teaspoons of salt.

Step 3: Splay fowl on table. Season with spice mixture.

Step 4: Stuff splayed pigeon inside partridge, partridge inside goose, goose inside turkey. Sew up triple-stuffed turkey. Set aside.

Step 5: Knead to a paste: 1 bushel flour and 10 pounds of butter. Roll out dough and put in large pie pan.

Step 6: Place turkey in middle of pan. Arrange woodcock, hare and hens around it.
Step 7: Cook 6 hours. Let cool. Serve.

CHRISTMAS DINNER WITH THE McCLURE EXPEDITION

(GREENLAND—1850)

Over the centuries, Christmas food and cheer have been shared in the unlikeliest places and the harshest climes. As further proof that the spirit of the season conquers all, Sir Robert McClure reported having this holiday feast with his cohorts aboard the *Investigator* off the coast of Greenland: Sandwich Island beef, musk veal from Prince of Wales' Strait, mincemeat from England, preserves from the Green Isle, and "dainty dishes from Scotland."

The following year, icebound on the Bay of Mercy, McClure and his men enjoyed plum pudding, Mercy Bay hare-soup, ptarmigan pasties, musk-ox jerky (hung from the rigging for two years)—and, the pièce de résistance: haunch of Banks Island reindeer.

After dessert and double allowances of grog, the explorers ventured outdoors and sang and danced on the polar ice under the Northern Lights.

CHRISTMAS DINNER IN SENEGAL, AFRICA

(1869)

This menu was printed in *The Chambers Journal* and was sent in by a British adventurer:

APPETIZER
"Snails from France, oysters torn from trees, fried locusts, and roasted crocodile eggs."

ENTRÉE
"Gazelle cutlets, stewed iguana, smoked elephant, manati breasts, hippo steaks, boiled alligator, monkeys on toast, land

crabs and Africa soles, carp, and mullet—detestable in themselves, but triumphant proof of the skill of the cook."

DESSERT
"Various fruits rejoicing in extraordinary shapes, long native names, and very nasty flavours."

CHRISTMAS DINNER WITH THE BRITISH ARMY

(SOUTH AFRICA—1885)

War correspondent Archibald Forbes enjoyed this menu at the encampment of the royal infantry on the Khyber Pass:

"Soup—Julienne. Fish—Whitebait from the Cabul River. Entrées—Cotelettes aux Champignons, Poulets a la Mayonaise. Joints—Ham and fowls, roast beef, roast saddle of mutton, boiled brisket of beef, boiled leg of mutton and caper sauce. Curry—chicken. Grilled sardines, cheese fritters. Sweets—Lemon jelly, blancmange, apricot tart, plum-pudding."

In a postscript to his account for *English Illustrated Magazine* Forbes added: "But truth compels the avowal that there was no table-linen, flowers, or silverware."

CHRISTMAS DINNER WITH THE U.S. ARMY

(SAUDI ARABIA—1990)

In 1990, the more than 300,000 soldiers of Operation Desert Shield enjoyed a 10-million-pound menu which consisted of: 75 tons of turkey, 86 tons of roast beef, 17 tons of shrimp, 210,000 pounds of fruitcake and pies, 224,000 pounds of bread and rolls, and thousands of gallons of eggnog and "Saudi champagne" (a sparkling nonalcoholic grape soda). There was more than enough to go around. Reported Attachment 111 battalion commander Major Bill Lucenta, after the holiday season, "I'm living out here in the middle of nowhere, and I've gained ten pounds since I got in-country."

CHRISTMAS DINNER WITH BILL AND HILLARY CLINTON

(1993)

This recent feast was held at the White House. Guests included the president's mother, the late Virginia Kelley, and her husband, Dick; the First Lady's mother, Dorothy; the president's brother, Roger, and his brother-in-law, Tony Rodham; plus Chelsea and Socks.

Though the dinner did not feature Pope John Paul passing almonds or Al Gore on a charger keeping order, it included:

ENTRÉE

Turkey and ham, cornbread stuffing, sweet potato casserole, mashed potatoes, green beans, broccoli, salad, green onions (Hillary's favorite), watermelon pickles, cranberry mold, and bing cherry mold.[3]

BEVERAGES

Wine, eggnog, syllabub (a frothy cream-and-wine concoction), and sweet-potato punch.[4]

DESSERT

Pumpkin pie (Chelsea's favorite), pecan pie (Mrs. Kelley's favorite), apple and cherry pie (the Rodhams' favorites).

[3]"Here we try everything," the First Lady told *New York Times* reporter Marian Burros ("A White House Christmas," *Newsweek,* 12-15-93).
[4]"Before you make a face, I'll send you a copy of the recipe [from an Arkansas newspaper]," the First Lady continued.

White House Holiday Treats

I n the left-hand column is a list of a holiday appetizers, entrées, desserts, and beverages—each associated with a certain president or First Lady. In the right-hand column is a list of the presidents and First Ladies. The two lists don't match up. Pin the holiday treat to the correct party.

HOLIDAY TREAT	PRESIDENT/ FIRST LADY
1. CHRISTMAS WALNUT-AND-SHERRY TURKEY According to this president's personal recipe: "Three days before the bird is slaughtered, it should have an English walnut forced down its throat three times a day, a glass of sherry once a day. The meat will be deliciously tender, and have a fine nutty flavor."	George Washington

2. DEER MEAT SAUSAGE — Nancy Reagan
This Western rancher's recipe called for half a deer, half a hog, and made 200 pounds of Christmas sausage.

3. CHRISTMAS TREE OF MEAT — Harry S. Truman
So many supporters showered this president-elect with Christmas food at his home in Marion, Ohio, he hung donated turkeys, opossums, capons, ducks, and geese from an apple tree in his backyard.

4. CHRISTMAS TREE COOKIES — Dolley Madison
The First Lady's own recipe with cinnamon, allspice, ginger, and melted chocolate.

5. SUGAR-FROSTED PINE TREE — Warren G. Harding
Baked by the chief executive's French chef, and decked with candy animals.

6. PRALINE ICE CREAM ON HOLLY LEAVES — Lady Bird Johnson
A Christmas Eve dessert from our youngest First Lady.

7. JUMBO JERSEY MINCE PIE — Benjamin Harrison
This was a gift of Jersey City bakers to our most prodigious president (300 lbs. plus). After a first Christmas pie mysteriously disappeared on the train from New York to Washington, a second was crated in a four-foot-square wooden box, secured with tenpenny nails, and dispatched to the White House with four guards sitting on each corner.

8. CALIFORNIA MONKEY BREAD — Pat Nixon
The First Lady's own down-home California recipe.

9. CINNAMON-LACED EGGNOG — Jackie Kennedy
A sinfully rich specialty of this First

Lady who later became the namesake of a famous ice cream.

10. NEW ENGLAND EGGNOG   Andrew Jackson

In the days before saturated fat intake became a concern, and DUI checkpoints were a thing of seasons future, this president's personal recipe called for: 1 dozen eggs, 1 quart cream, 1 quart milk, 1 pint brandy, ½ pint rye, ¼ pint sherry, ¼ pint Jamaican or New England rum.

11. CHRISTMAS EGG BALL SOUP   William Howard Taft

A Christmas Day appetizer for the president who always said: "If you can't take the heat, stay out of the kitchen."

ANSWER KEY:

1.	Christmas Walnut-and-Sherry Turkey	Benjamin Harrison (1889)
2.	Deer Meat Sausage	Lyndon and Lady Bird Johnson (1965)
3.	Christmas Tree of Meat	Warren G. Harding (1920)
4.	Christmas Tree Cookies	Pat Nixon (1972)
5.	Sugar-Frosted Pine Tree	Andrew Jackson (1835)
6.	Praline Ice Cream on Holly Leaves	Jackie Kennedy (1962)
7.	Jumbo Jersey Mince Pie	William Howard Taft (1909)
8.	California Monkey Bread	Nancy Reagan (1983)
9.	Cinnamon-Laced Eggnog	Dolley Madison (1811)
10.	New England Eggnog	George Washington (1790)
11.	Christmas Egg Ball Soup	Harry S. Truman (1952)

Astronomic Gastronomic

As we have seen, Christmas fare, even in the leanest of times, has rarely come in Jenny Craig portions. Here are the season's champion pies, puddings, and crackers:

WORLD'S LARGEST MINCE PIE

Baked in 1780 for Sir Henry Gray, this pie weighed 165 pounds, measured 9 feet across, and was transported from the bakery to Sir Henry's by oxcart.

AMERICA'S LARGEST MINCE PIE

Baked for the crew of Pennsylvania Railroad Train #273-283 at their Third Annual Christmas Festival in 1901, this specimen measured 4 feet across, 6 inches deep, and was delivered hot by horse-driven wagon compliments of a wealthy New Jersey commuter.

ENGLAND'S LARGEST CHICKEN POTPIE

The entrée at St. John's Church Christmas Fair of 1871 contained 100 chickens and took four hale and hardy men to carry to the table.

WALL STREET'S LARGEST PLUM PUDDING

A 600-pound dessert was delivered to the Consolidated Exchange the Friday before Christmas, 1909. Brokers stopped work, played football on the floor of the exchange; then, appetite whetted, devoured the prodigious pudding in short order.

LARGEST "FUNCTIONAL" CHRISTMAS CRACKER

According to *Guinness*, a 150-foot-long, 10-foot-diameter cookie was exhibited and consumed at Westfield Shopping Town in Sydney, Australia, on November 9, 1991.

LARGEST CHRISTMAS DONUT PARADE FLOAT

The Dunkin' Donuts float in the 1994 Macy's Parade was a North Pole donut factory measuring 34 feet long, 22 feet wide, and 21 feet tall. Run by "Fred the Baker," the float was trimmed with 20-pound donuts, a massive donut clock, and a rooftop studded with 28 colorful donuts and sweetrolls.

Leftovers!
The Donald's 500-Pound
Doggie Bag

New York, 1993: Donald Trump and his bride, Marla Maples, gave five hundred pounds of leftovers from their Christmastime wedding reception to the Brooklyn Senior Citizens Center. The more than one thousand guests~including Mayor David Dinkins, Howard Stern, Whitney Houston, Arnold Schwarzenegger, Don King, Joe Frazier, and Saudi financier Adnan Khoshoggi~ were unable to clean their plates. The donated leftovers included steak, ribs, salmon, lamb, curried shrimp, and a large helping of the Trumps' six-tier wedding cake.

Goose & Gastro Final

Now, our last course: True-Falses, Multiples, and Fill-ins covering everything but the kitchen sink:

1. How big was the prize turkey Scrooge bought for the Cratchits?
   a. Half the size of Tiny Tim.
   b. About the same size as Tiny Tim.
   c. Twice the size of Tiny Tim.
   d. 28 lbs. 4 oz.
   e. Dickens doesn't say.
2. What beverage did all of the Cratchits, including the five youngsters, drink on Christmas Day?

DOUBLE JEOPARDY
3. Scrooge had a nip before he saw the ghost of his business partner, Jacob Marley. True or false?
4. In 1967, London police, in an effort to curb holiday drinking and driving, administered breath tests at checkpoints throughout the city. As a result, the auto accident figures from the previous year were reduced by 10 percent. True or false?

5. In 1994, Ireland's Environment Minister, Michael Smith, toughened holiday drink-and-drive laws. As a result he had what he called "a very difficult Christmas," receiving "ferocious and abusive" calls and letters from Irishmen, as well as a number of death threats. True or false?

6. According to a study conducted by the Department of Psychiatry and Behavioral Sciences at the University of Southern California, the ratio of men to women who deal with holiday depression by drinking or taking drugs is:
    a. 5:1.
    b. 1:5.
    c. 1:1.
    The ratio of women to men who deal with holiday depression by eating is:
    a. 3:1.
    b. 1:3.
    c. 1:1.

7. Last season a Korean company stocked vending machines in Korea and Japan with fruitcakes from Our Lady of Guadeloupe Trappist Abbey, which produces a gourmet 3-pound fruitcake containing 120-proof brandy. True or false?

8. Identify the popular Japanese alternative to Christmas plum pudding.

9. In 1980, Charles T. Powers, *Los Angeles Times* Nairobi bureau chief, had Christmas dinner with the Mau-Mau in Kenya. The Mau-Mau holiday menu featured:
    a. *Points d'éléphant*, and Plum Pudding *Sans Réproche*.
    b. Braised Breast of Afrikaner, with cranberry mold.
    c. Turkey and roast beef with Yorkshire pudding.
    d. Hippo steaks, boiled alligator, and monkeys on toast.

10. Of all the Christmas MREs (meals ready to eat) issued to the multinational peacekeeping force in Somalia in 1992, those issued by the Italian Army were the most popular. Some American, British, and French soldiers were ready to swap anything for an Italian MRE. Why?

11. *Artichoke fritters with bearnaise sauce, rigatoni and linguine, Southern fried chicken, tiramisu, and ice cream sundaes.*

This was a recent Christmas luncheon menu of what daytime talk-show star for the producers of his or her show:

a. Maury Povich.

b. Marilu.

c. Geraldo.

d. Oprah Winfrey.

e. Rikki Lake.

12. According to Neel Lattimore, a spokeswoman for Mrs. Clinton, the First Cat, Socks, was banned from the State Dining Room in the 1993 season. Why?

13. The average American is said to gain four to six pounds over the holiday season. Figuring for a population of 256 million, how many pounds did we gain as a nation last Christmas?

EXTRA CREDIT

Who Said It?

1. "Making [Christmas] chocolate chip cookies is an enormously fulfilling task for children; they eat the chips, they eat the dough, and they argue about the size of the cookies."

a. Mr. Rogers.

b. Dr. Spock.

c. Tipper Gore.

d. Hillary Clinton.

2. "It [the bowl of reindeer stew] is great. I highly recommend it."

a. Jimmy Carter.

b. Ronald Reagan.

c. Richard Nixon.

d. Bill Clinton.

3. "While the monkeys were roasting over our campfire, I told my porters the story of Jesus' mysterious and magical birth."

a. Yul Gibbons.

b. Pat Robertson.

c. Douchan Gersi.

d. Ted Nugent.

4. "Having thus aroused the family, they would enter the domicile with stamping and scramble to the blazing fire, greedily eating the praetzilles and schnickilies, imbibe, with many a rugged

joke and ringing peal of laughter, heavy draughts of liquor, and then with many a screech and holler rush into the night to visit the next neighbor."
  a. John A. Chapman, speaking of Yule festivity in the Old South.
  b. Jesse Helms.
  c. Jesse Jackson.
  d. Loretta Lynn.

5. "The proper behavior all through the holiday season is to be drunk. This drunkenness culminates on New Year's Eve, when you get so drunk you kiss the person you're married to."
  a. Don Johnson.
  b. Tom Arnold.
  c. Mickey Rourke.
  d. P. J. O'Rourke.
  e. Norman Mailer.

ANSWER KEY:
  1. c. "Twice the size of Tiny Tim."
  2. Hot gin and lemons in a jug.

Double Jeopardy:
  3. False. He only had some gruel. And after his conversion by the three spirits of Christmas, Scrooge pledged to live by "The Total Abstinence Principle."
  4. False. They were reduced by 50 percent.
  5. True.
  6. a. 5:1. a. 3:1.
  7. False. Though the Korean company approached Our Lady of Guadeloupe Fruitcakes for vending machine inventory, Father Richard, the business manager, declined to fill the order, saying, "We really don't like anything that smacks of big business."
  8. Fujiya's "French-style" strawberry shortcake (traditionally served with a plastic fir tree on top).
  9. c. Turkey and roast beef with Yorkshire pudding.
  10. The Italian MRE contained a much sought-after "Cordiale."
  11. d. Oprah Winfrey.

12. The puss reportedly had his eye on the 100-pound gingerbread White House built by First Pastry Chef, Roland Mesnier.
13. National Christmas weight gain, 1994: 1.28 trillion pounds. (256 million people X 5-pound average holiday weight gain per person)

Extra Credit:
1. d. Hillary Clinton.
2. d. Bill Clinton, after eating the dish at the Downtown Deli and Cafe, a restaurant near Anchorage, Alaska, during the 1994 holiday season
3. c. Douchan Gersi, author/adventurer, on having Christmas dinner with Borneo headhunters in 1978.
4. a. John A. Chapman, from his 1892 account of Yule festivity in South Carolina.
5. d. P. J. O'Rourke.

VI.

Here Comes Santa Claus!

St. Nick: Yesterday & Today

His eyes~how they twinkled! His dimples, how merry!

His cheeks were like roses, his nose like a cherry!

He had a broad face, and a little round belly,

That shook when he laugh'd, like a bowlful of jelly!

—Clement C. Moore, "A Visit from St. Nicholas" (1823)

Physically, mentally, spiritually, I'm wonderful.

Financially I need the stamps.

—Winfred Eugene Holley, seventy-five, who legally changed his name
to Santa Claus in 1982, and lives on Social Security off-season

The wages for a Santa are very low~dirt cheap.

After twelve years in the business, my

top pay was $12,000, and that is nothing

compared to what the job requires.

—LeRoy Scholtz, fifty-three, who legally changed his name to "Santa C. Claus"
in 1978, and who spends the off-season in Bermuda

Santa Clauses seem a lot seedier than they used to.

—Andy Rooney

The Nick
of Time

S aint Nicholas was born seventeen centuries ago in the town of Parara, Asia Minor, near Turkey. Pure and self-sacrificing even as an infant, he only nursed from his mother after sundown and restricted himself to one breast.

When he grew up he became the bishop of Myra. But his career was interrupted when Emperor Diocletian imprisoned him for refusing to bow down before Roman gods. According to one report the saint narrowly escaped being eaten by lions in the coliseum of Nicomedia.

On his return home as an ex-con, Nick revived three boys who'd been chopped up and salt-pickled by a local butcher; tossed three sacks of gold through the window and into the stockings of the dowryless daughters of a poor pawnbroker; and he came to blows with Arius, king of the Arians, at the Nicaean ecclesiastical council of 314 for questioning the immaculate birth of our Lord. While attending this council, his donkey was decapitated by robbers, and he magically restored the animal to life. Returning to his diocese in Myra by ship, he encountered a terrible storm, was thrown overboard, and sailed safely to shore in his hat.

On the merit of these and other marvelous acts, Nick was

named patron saint of pawnbrokers, maidens, mariners, kids, and, for undisclosed reasons, thieves as well. Finally, after receiving many other decorations and honors, in the year 342, December 6, he gave up the ghost.

Supposedly.

There was no news of him for more than seven centuries. Nothing seemed to be stirring, not even a mouse. Then a slight disturbance: in 1082, the saint's mortal remains were exhumed in Myra and spirited to the Shrine of San Nicola, in Bari, Italy, by forty-seven Italian businessman. A little while later another commercially minded Italian, Columbus, discovered Haiti and, in memory of Nick's storm-besieged voyage in his hat, dedicated a port to him.

In the next centuries, more churches and shrines in Europe were dedicated to Nicholas than to any other saint. His popularity in the Middle Ages was second only to that of Jesus and Mary. In his honor and in his name, nuns began to distribute candy to children on December 6. His mausoleum at San Nicola became the destination of many a pilgrimage, since legend had it that his body secreted a medicinal myrrh-scented philter which instantly healed the blind, the lame, and the diseased.

Things went on like this for some time: the pilgrimages, the dedications, the distribution of candy.

Finally in the early eighteenth century, the most miraculous event of all: our hero resurfaced in Bavaria in white beard and red woolen suit. Soon he was traveling far and wide, throughout the continent and across the seas, as we see now from our Nick Nut & Dateline:

1700   The Germans resurrect St. Nick as Kris Kringle, a.k.a. Santa Claus, and bring him to the New World.

1753   St. Nicholas is built, the first church in New York City. (Later, relics from the saint are installed at the Greek Orthodox church: a piece of his casket, clothing, myrrh from his bones, a piece of his skull.)

1823   Dr. Clement Clarke Moore, professor at New York Theological Seminary, pens "A Visit from St. Nicholas," a poem for his kids. The *Troy Sentinel* prints it; the piece becomes an overnight sensation.

1863   Thomas Nast, cartoonist for *Harper's Weekly*, turns Santa

into a chubby, rosy-cheeked chimney jumper. (Formerly
he was only slightly chubby and used front doors.)[1]

1897 Eight-year-old Virginia O'Hanlon asks the *New York Sun*
if there is a Santa Claus. The *Sun* replies with a resound-
ing yes! (For the other side of the issue, see "The Claus
Controversy," page 176.)

1912 The first true flying Claus lands a double-winged "aero-
plane" in San Francisco's Golden Gate Park on Christmas Day and distributes toys to thousands of kids.

1939 Robert May, a Montgomery Ward adman, gives Santa
Rudolph, the Red-Nosed Reindeer, to lead Dasher, Donder, Dancer, Prancer, and the rest of his team.

1947 *Miracle on 34th Street* premieres. Santa Claus (Edmund
Gwenn) proves to Natalie Wood, age seven, that he
exists. Gwenn receives an Oscar for his performance.

Here ended what Santaologists refer to as their man's "golden
period." This was followed by his "post-modern" stage, highlighted
by these religious, political, and commercial developments:

1970 The Catholic Church, under Pope Paul VI, officially
drops St. Nick as a major saint.

1972–78 Hare Krishnas throughout the U.S. are arrested for collecting holiday contributions, dressed as Santas, without
permits.[2]

1981 The Rent-a-Santa industry booms. More than 13,000 are
rented during the season. (See "Have Gut Will Travel,"
page 197.)

1982 Winfred Eugene Holley, seventy-five, former civilian
contractor for the Air Force, legally changes his name to
Santa Claus. (See "The Men Who Would Be Kringle,"
page 193.)

---

[1] In addition to the modern Santa, Nast also created the Democratic donkey and
Republic elephant.
[2] Most arrests were on misdemeanor charges. But in Kansas City, 1977, Hare Krishna
follower Robert S. Edell, dressed as a Santa Claus, was arrested after he and an "elf"
allegedly assaulted Salvation Army rep Elizabeth Batarseh for attempting to claim
their street corner.

1985   The torch is lit for the first Annual Santa Claus Olympics in Union Square, New York City.

1986   Reverend Romano Ferraro of St. John Vianney Roman Catholic Church in Colonia, New Jersey, tells parish children that Santa Claus is dead and that there is no North Pole toy factory or Rudolph, the Red-Nosed Reindeer. A diocese spokesman retracts the statement and apologizes for Father Ferraro's "zeal." (See "The Anti-Clauses," page 226.)

1990   The Los Angeles chapter of the Underwater Photographic Society holds their first Annual Santa Claus Dive off Catalina Island.

1990   At the Okonite Corporation, North Brunswick, New Jersey, 123 employees are suspended from work for refusing to take off their Santa hats.

1993   Carl Malamud, president of the Internet Multicasting Service of Washington, becomes the first on-line computer Santa. He interfaces electronically with more than ten thousand youngsters.

1994   A handwritten, signed copy of Clement Clarke Moore's 1823 poem "A Visit from St. Nicholas" fetches $255,500 at Christie's auction. (Pre-auction estimates of value ranged from $70,000 to $90,000.)

1994   Thirty Nicks from ten different countries compete in the Santa Claus World Cup in Drammen, Norway. Events include: Fence and Rooftop Climbing, Chimney Sliding, and Caroling. The judges were eight-year-olds in elf costumes.

1994   Forty Santas meet for the annual National Congress of the Santa Claus Trade Union in Norway. Santas unanimously vote to boycott any country that eats reindeer. The vote is repealed when the group realizes Norway is one.

The Santa Stats[3]

- Percentage of American children between three and ten years old who believe in Santa: 87 percent.
- Percentage of American households that leave milk and cookies out for him: 10 percent.
- Percentage of American children who say they saw him last Christmas: 8 percent.
- Percentage of American child psychologists who advise parents of preschool children to "confirm Santa's existence": 40 percent.
- Percentage of French adults who support belief in Santa Claus because he gives their children "a chance to dream": 84 percent.
- Percentage of French adults who think "it is totally idiotic to make a child believe in someone that does not exist": 12 percent (undecided: 4 percent).

[3]Sources: *The New York Times, The Wall Street Journal.*

To Be or Not to Be: The Claus Controversy

A s we see from the North Poll, the jury is still out on the age-old question of Santa's existence. The debate arose more than a hundred years ago, and the battle lines of yea- and naysayers were quickly drawn.

The most strident voice in the second camp was that of Reverend A. B. Grosh who in 1854 proclaimed: " 'Kris Kringle'—this is a horridly barbarous imitation of a German barbarism, into which an English ear has led many of our newspaper editors and writers. It is neither English nor bad German, but a mere jargon or gibberish of the vilest kind—and when the facts are known, sounds like ribaldry!"

Soon Francis P. Church, editor of the *New York Sun*, countered with his famous words to a bewildered eight-year-old little girl. "Yes, Virginia, there is a Santa Claus . . . Alas! how dreary would be the world if there were no Santa Claus. It would be as dreary as if there were no Virginia!"

More than a century has gone by and now the voices of a new generation of Claus commentators, critics, and professionals have entered the debate.

Now, the *Just Say Noel!* open forum on the thorniest and most persistent question of the season: once and for all—

DOES SANTA EXIST?

No, Gretchen and Stacy, there is no such man.
—Alan N. MacLeese, columnist for the Flint, Michigan, *Journal*, in reply to
two girls who asked the same question in 1975

*Horse spit. Santa Claus isn't a lie. He's a legend who symbolizes
the spirits of unconditional love and generosity and happiness . . .
Despite the fact that the jolly old fat man is now deemed a
danger to society by the oh-so-politically correct, I will personally unplug
the Christmas lights of anyone who tries to set my boy straight.*
—Michael Burkett, syndicated columnist of "The Dad Zone," and father
of a third-grader who still believes in Santa

*I never believed in Mr. Claus, but remember humoring my parents.
I thought, "How long are they going to keep this up?"*
—Quentin Crisp, eighty-five, expatriate British writer, born on Christmas Day

Santa Claus is a white man's invention.
—Representative Adam Clayton Powell, 1963

*When they stand back and stare, I know I'm going to get the
"Santa isn't black" line.*
—Calvin Neal, 1993, a black Santa in Kansas City for eighteen years

*I had one kid saying, "Santa's not Chinese." And I said, "You're right.
Santa is not Chinese. He's Hawaiian."*
—San Francisco Santa Claus Patrick Landeza, a self-described
"Hawaiian-Filipino-Chinese-Irish-Spanish-Guamian," who wishes Filipino
children a Merry Christmas in Tagalog, and plays ukulele on his throne

*"Santy" Claus. We called him "Santy" because that's what "Auntie" Bella
called him. I really believed he came. In some ways I still do.*
—Larry King, 1993

Santa isn't coming. He's just breathing hard.
—Anonymous

The final and decisive word on the holiday debate must go to Jean Jones, a housewife from Kansas City, who last season made a statement even the Grinch himself couldn't rebut. "We have a motto at our house," Mrs. Jones told a reporter. "If you don't believe, you don't receive. And so my children, who are now adults in their thirties, have never admitted there's no Santa Claus."

Missives
to the Man
Up North

After much dispute, the court case against Kris Kringle in *Miracle on 34th Street* was finally decided in the defendant's favor based on kids' North Pole letters to him delivered by legal authority of the U.S. Postal Service.

"Since the United States of America believes this man to be Santa Claus, this Court will not dispute it. Case dismissed!" declared Judge Harper.

Today, in addition to the more than seven hundred thousand letters which the U.S. Postal Service hefts to the Pole every season, many kids are now e-mailing their Man, his elves, and Rudolph himself on the Information Superhighway. Alternatively, those who prefer a live long-distance toll call to the saint ($10 for ten minutes, $25 for half hour; Family and Friends discount not applicable) have taken advantage of Sprint's direct line to his Workshop.

But communiqués to Father Christmas—whether they come by post or wire—have changed in the course of the last hundred years, as the following examples show:

GOLDEN AGE LETTERS

Christmas, 1900 (New York)

Dear Mr. Santa Claus:

I hope you'll pay 'tention. I want a soldier hat and a sword and gun.

P.S. Please don't fill up the toe of my stocking with peanuts as you did last year.

P.P.S. If you wouldn't mind leaving my things before I go to bed I'll be much obliged.

Allen Starr
[dictated to his mother]

Christmas, 1901 (Detroit)

Dear Santa Claus:

I Havent Had Any Christmas Tree in 4 Years And I Have Broken My Trimmings And I Want A Pair of Roller Skates And A Book, I Cant Think of Any Thing More. I Want You To Think Of Something More. Good By.

Edsel Ford, 8 [son of Henry and Clara Ford, future president of Ford Motor Co.]

NEW AGE LETTERS

Christmas, 1986 (California)

Dear Santa:

I would like some brains and to look cute. But if you cannot make me cute, I will just take the brains.

Anonymous

Christmas, 1993 (California)

Dear Santa:

Thank you for replacing my broken doll last year. I didn't mean to pull her head off. Her legs were another accident. Well her arms, that is another story. Her hair got caught in the scissors, it wasn't her day!

Anonymous

Christmas, 1993 (California)

Dear Santa:

All I want is money and I want it now.

Thanks, Kim.

P.S. S.A.S.E. enclosed. No checks please.[4]

Our final communiqué, also from the Golden State, proves that St. Nick doesn't just hear from the nice nowadays, but also from the once naughty:

Christmas, 1994 (Folsom State Penitentiary)

Dear Santa:

I am in prison because I was a bad boy, but now I am a good boy. Would you please bring me the following items for Christmas:

One getaway car and driver, one jackhammer, one pair of bolt cutters. Oh, yeah, and a rubber suit so I don't get shocked on the electric fence. If you can't, I'll settle for a blow-up doll.

Thank you, Ronny.

P.S. I believe in you, Santa!

---

[4] The last two notes were sent to "The Crying Santa," Bruce McGuy, a thirty-seven-year-old San Jose contractor, who dresses up as St. Nick every season and answers mail. The letters are collected in his *Even Santa Claus Cries Sometimes*, from Home Run Publishing Co., San Jose, California. His 1995 sequel is entitled *Even Santa Laughs Sometimes*.

Santa's M.O.:
Five Theories of
Kindergartners

Santa Claus was in my house! Putting presents for me under our tree!
While eight flying reindeer were on my roof! I was so awestruck
I wet my bed. This incident did not leave me with deep emotional scars or
make me hate my parents when the truth was ultimately revealed.
But it did give me a whole new standard of excitement.
—Michael Burkett, columnist

I n spite of the persistent skepticism about his existence in certain circles, many children still insist that they have had a Close Encounter of the Third Kind with St. Nick. But most are divided on the subject of exactly how he gets into their house without being apprehended by the grown-ups.

A few seasons ago, some New Orleans kindergartners aired their theories about this[5]:

[5]Source: *Los Angeles Times*, 12-25-84.

THE GOPHER THEORY

*Santa digs a hole in the ground like a gopher and then
tunnels his way under the house. He doesn't get muddy because
I clean out under the house for him.*
—Jason Gendusa

THE ROLLERBLADE THEORY

Santa puts on skates, crashes in, and makes a new door.
—Anthony Lama

THE KAMIKAZE THEORY

He and the reindeers bust the roof without making any noise.
—Leah Collums

THE COVERT OPERATIVE THEORY

*He uses the chimney, except we give him the burglar alarm number so he
can turn it off so we won't think he's a bad person.*
—Melissa Culotta

THE BYO BRICK THEORY

*We don't have a chimney, so Santa makes one. He carries all the bricks
with him and it takes him about an hour.*
—Vincent Antoine

Santa Surprises
to the Stars

Who can forget their favorite gift from St. Nick?

Here are some famous people and some of the greatest surprises they found under the tree in Christmases past from the "Santa" in their lives.

We start with toys, and end with what so many kids dream of, no matter the age—wheels:

TOYS

SANTA	KID	SURPRISE
Queen Victoria's Mom (1836)	Queen Victoria (age 17)	Two Dresden china dolls.
Queen Latifah's Parents	Queen Latifah (singer, star of *Living Single*)	Lego set (Remembers Queen Latifah: "I got it every year for like, three years—8, 9, 10. I was a Lego fiend.")

President of Nigeria (1984)	President Reagan	Silver medallion gaming pieces
President Bush (1991)	His grandkids	"Slime" (Said the president while shopping in a Frederick, Maryland, mall: "We've got a little toy department to look at to get some stuff for the grandchildren. 'Slime' is the name of it, I believe. It's a toy.")
Vice President Gore (1992)	Tipper	Red drum set (The Second Lady told *Ladies' Home Journal* it was her favorite Christmas present ever. She has played drums since she was fourteen.)
Larry King's parents (1935–36)	Larry	Erector set and Lincoln Logs (Recalls King: "My Erector set. I got it when I was 8. . . . Lincoln Logs. I was 9. You could build anything with them.")
Steve Buscemi's parents	Steve (actor, *Reservoir Dogs*)	Ventriloquist dummy, Jerry Mahoney (his favorite Christmas toy, given him at age 9)
Antonio Banderas' Parents	Antonio (vampire in *Interview with a Vampire*)	Balloons

WHEELS

SANTA	KID	SURPRISE
Disney Studio (1994)	Tim Allen (star of studio's hit, *The Santa Clause*)	$75,000 Porsche
Allman Brothers (1992)	Jon Podell (their agent)	Harley chopper
Oprah Winfrey (1993)	Beverly (her producer)	Jeep Grand Cherokee (The gift was presented to Beverly accompanied by the song "I'm Every Woman.")
John Travolta (1992)	His assistant	Triumph sports car

Ho-Ho-Hollywood

Some of the most memorable Santas and Santa sayings come to us from the capital of holiday jolliness and make-believe. Here are a selection of movie and TV Santaisms from Christmases past. Pin the lefthand bon mot to the right holiday show:

SANTAISM

1. "You relinquish any previous identity, real or implied."

2. "If I didn't know you were Flintstone, I'd think you were me."

MOVIE/TV SHOW

A). Intern at Bellevue Mental Hospital to Doris, who asks if Santa Claus has checked in.
Miracle on 34th Street

B). A burnt-out Santa (Paul Lynde) to a bartender (Andy Griffith) who serves him spiked milk.
Glen Campbell Goodtime Hour

3. "Oh please, there's only one fat guy that brings us presents, and his name ain't Santa."

C). Charlie Brown's sister, Sally, in a letter to Santa dictated to Charlie.
Charlie Brown Christmas

4. "Why, there are *thousands* of Santa Clauses down there! . . . We'll just take one. The earthlings won't miss him."

D). Buddy, Harry's crazy father, about a certain acquaintance of his from the asylum.
Night Court

5. "I can offer you a Robin Hood, two Napoleons, and a Rasputin, but no Santa Claus."

E). The Santa Clause on a card in the pocket of Santa's suit, found by Tim Allen after St. Nick falls off his roof and dies.
The Santa Clause

6. "Nick—Santa Claus? That's hysterical . . . Though it would explain the red convertible. It flies."

F). Santa Kramer to his boss, who fires him for complaining about low wages and talking Communism to his elves.
Seinfeld

7. "Can you see my boobs?"

G). Martian Commander Kemar, on a mission to kidnap Santa and bring him back to his planet to make Martian kids happy.
Santa Claus Conquers the Martians

8. "You can't fire me. I'm Santa!"

H). Roseanne, in her Santa suit, to her sister, Jackie, playing Mrs. Claus.
Roseanne

9. "Why can't I be just like the Easter bunny and drop a couple eggs on the lawn and beat it?"

I). Santa Claus to Fred Flint-stone, who puts on his suit and fills in for him after Santa falls off a Bedrock roof and sprains his ankle. *A Flintstone Christmas*

10. "If it seems too complicated, make it easy on yourself. Just send money. How about tens and twenties?"

J). Bart Simpson, to his mother. *The Simpsons*

ANSWER KEY:

1. E. *The Santa Clause*.
2. I. *A Flintstone Christmas*.
3. J. *The Simpsons*.
4. G. *Santa Claus Conquers the Martians*.
5. A. *Miracle on 34th Street*.
6. D. *Night Court*.
7. H. *Roseanne*.
8. F. *Seinfeld*.
9. B. *Glen Campbell Goodtime Hour*, with Paul Lynde.
10. C. *A Charlie Brown Christmas*.

Claus
Incognito

I n recent seasons some saints have concealed their true identities, taking no credit for their generosity and magical deeds. Here now is a Who's Who of a few real-life drive-by-night Santas of the modern age—men who have materialized every Yule from Skid Row to Vallejo to the Capital of Country Music, dropped surprises, and disappeared with a flash of light.

THE CADILLAC SANTA OF L.A.

He first surfaced in the Midnight Mission district of Los Angeles' Skid Row on Christmas Eve, 1984, wearing a silk Italian suit. He doled out thousands in ten-dollar bills to the homeless, chatting with them while doing so, but refusing to answer questions about his identity. Clancy Imislund, manager of the Skid Row mission, gave this description of the Cadillac Santa to the *Los Angeles Times* in 1991: "He drove up in his brand-new Eldorado—he has a new one every year—with three nervous elfs—they obviously work for him—and said, 'Get 'em ready.' And then he started giving out money." He ran out of funds within a few minutes. "The banks closed and he didn't have enough for everyone in the streets," Imislund explained. "He was real apologetic."

THE ELDORADO SANTA OF L.A.

When the Cadillac Santa passed away in 1992, he was replaced by a man who identified himself only as "Cadillac Santa's Elf." He drove a new cherry red Eldorado into the Midnight Mission at Christmastime, 1993, and gave out ten dollar bills to all comers. When Skid Row residents saw the Cadillac arrive the next season, they cried, "The ten-dollar man is here! The ten-dollar man is here!" and hurried to out to wish him a Merry Christmas.

The Eldorado Santa is rumored to be Ronald Moran, an eighty-year-old L.A. car dealer. He declines to talk about himself, but has these words about his predecessor: "The Cadillac Santa said there were three stages of wealth. The first stage is when you make it. The second stage is fighting to keep it. The third stage is when you give it all away. That is the most enjoyable stage."

VALLEJO'S FAMOUS
HITCHHIKING SANTA

His real name is Sparky Brager, he's forty-eight, and off-season he washes dishes at Denny's and collects disability payments. In-season, donning a beard, rubber boots, and a Santa suit, he hitchhikes around the Western states and distributes candy to kids. So motorists can readily identify him he wears this sign on his red windbreaker:

VALLEJO'S FAMOUS HITCHHIKING SANTA,
28TH YEAR. SINCE NOV. 23, 1966

Instead of a sack he carries an old avocado green suitcase with a portrait of a rosy-cheeked Nick and the message: "Donations appreciated. Proceeds used for food, lodging, travel. (Not connected with Toys for Tots.)"

"Everybody has a calling, and this is mine," Vallejo's Famous

Hitchhiking Santa told a reporter last season while stopping on the road not for milk and cookies but for a Ben's Big Burger. "I'm going to do this until I can't walk anymore. I just want people to show more love and happiness in the world." Then he added, "I love it. Bringing joy to the kids. I'm no kook in a red suit!"

CAPRICE CLASSIC CLAUS
OF NASHVILLE

A few years ago, Doug and Patty Brown's car broke down Christmas Eve. A 1986 Caprice Classic pulled up and its driver offered them a lift. On the ride home, Doug and Patty told the driver they couldn't afford to get their car fixed. Pulling up to their house, he handed them the keys to the Caprice. Patty, who thought she recognized the samaritan at that point, said, "Are you Garth Brooks?" The composer of "Ropin' the Wind" shook his head, smiled, and said "No, but I'm a big fan." Then he told them to have a Merry Christmas and to enjoy the Caprice.

The Men Who
Would Be
Kringle: A Tale
of Two Santas

SANTA C. CLAUS OF PA[6]

LeRoy Scholtz originally worked as a mailman in Kansas. He first put on the beard, boots, and big red for Sears in Wichita, 1968. He transferred to Santa's Workshop in North Pole, Colorado; then to Santa's Village in Cherokee, North Carolina; and finally to Santa's Workshop in North Pole, New York.

"He worked here for nine years," LeRoy's last Pole employer, Robert R. Reiss, told *The New York Times*. "As each year passed he got more and more into the character, became more and more eccentric. He lives that role of Santa now. It's his whole life."

At the end of his tenure up north, Scholtz drove to Plattsburgh and filed for a name change. But the judge nixed "Santa Claus," saying that the name had to be protected. Scholtz remained optimistic, and did not give up. "I am 99 percent Santa Claus. We're still working on the case and we'll be back."

[6]Source: "Claus Leaves North Pole Seeking Job Opportunity," *The New York Times*, 12-19-79.

Meantime he changed the name on his bank account and union card to "Santa C. Claus," and he bought a red Chevy convertible with plates that read SANTA 1. Then, serving his notice at the Pole, he drove his sleigh to Bethlehem, Pennsylvania, and there began freelancing at hospitals, malls, and holiday charity functions. His fee: $1,000 a day, plus expenses and retainer for his booking agent.

When the *Times* asked Santa C. about his postseason itinerary he replied, "I'm putting my reindeer out to pasture and flying to Bermuda."

SANTA CLAUS OF L.A.[7]

Winfred Eugene Holley was originally an Air Force civilian contractor from Kissimmee, Florida. Of his conversion and career change, he told the *Los Angeles Times* in 1982, "I was in Calgary one summer in a white safari suit and everyone kept saying, 'Hi, Santa Claus!' I went back to the hotel and looked in the mirror and even I could see a resemblance."

So he turned pro. But after several seasons the wanna-bes in the business started to dampen his spirits. "It was sad to see these derelicts and high school kids stuffed with pillows. So I got to kicking it around and I decided I wanted to be Santa Claus all the time."

Holley moved to Los Angeles and successfully filed for a name change. Then he hired an agent, ordered new stationery, took an L.A. North Pole P.O. box, and bought a 1960 Cadillac convertible sleigh.

In the 1982 season, America's first and only legal Santa Claus[8] received more than ten thousand letters. "Ninety percent were just plain greedy," he reported. "There is a world of difference between the greedy and the needy, but I loved the little greedy monsters, too."

He responded to all, even the little girl from Las Vegas who included a snapshot of herself straddling the hood of a Rolls-Royce,

[7]Source: "Santa Claus, The Real McCoy," *Los Angeles Times*, 12-16-82.
[8]In 1994 Terry Randolph, a forty-three-year-old rental Nick from Iowa, also officially changed his name and became America's second fully legal "Santa Claus."

and who asked for everything in the Smurf catalog, plus an 18-karat gold necklace.

Of his personal life since conversion, Santa says he has given up drink, cigarettes, and cursing. "I've become so nice I don't have any fun myself. Not like Holley had." In spite of the sacrifice, he adds with a chuckle, "I've had not one regret, and I never will."

But he ended last season with one regret after all. He had to sue a resort in Park City, Utah, for nonpayment of $6,732, his retainer for thirty-four days of work. "Santa isn't supposed to sue people," he told *People* magazine. "But what choice did I have? I need stamps." The resort counter-sued Santa Holley for $10,270.80, the cost of his hotel room and long-distance phone calls. "I'm already looking like the Grinch in this thing," said Barbara Zimonja, the president of Resort Group. "And Christmas is my favorite holiday."

Profile of the Average Rental Santa[9]

Height: 6'

Weight: 220 pounds

Waist: 39 ½"

Age: 44

Education: 63 percent have college degrees

Children: 3.2

Languages: 21 percent are multilingual; 29 percent use sign

[9]Source: Homart Mall Santa Survey, 1992

Have Gut Will Travel: The Rent-a-Santa Industry

It's always very difficult to get Santas. We're out there busting our butts on this."
—Santa supplier for a national distributor

If I see a Santa look-alike at a bus stop, I'll pull over. One elderly man I approached said he was going to shave off his beard because he couldn't take it anymore. He was out here for a mellow vacation and everyone was hitting on him.
—Cathy Perks, manager for nation's leading Santa supplier,
Western Temporary Services, Tustin, Texas

Santa is a sex symbol to some women . . . especially those who have had a drink or two at parties."
—Ralph Gertz, sixty-one, a veteran Cleveland Santa, to *Playboy* magazine

Now, Everything You Ever Wanted to Know about rental Santas—but were too young to ask:

- How many rental Santas currently work in the U.S. during the holiday season?
  About 20,000 (up 200 percent from 1972).

- What is the wage scale for a Los Angeles Kmart Claus, versus a Macy's?
  Kmart : $5 to 9 per hour. Macy's: up to $18 per hour (with "under-the-sleigh" tips).

- Who is the highest-paid Santa?
  Brady White. Twelve years ago, he was an unemployed Los Angeles actor. Now he gets $4,000 for a photo shoot in the Swiss Alps, and once received $80,000 for a television commercial. He drives a red Mercedes with SANTA plates, his beard is insured by Lloyd's of London, and he has met everyone from Pope John Paul II to Madonna. He declines to reveal his annual income, only saying: "It feeds the reindeer and the elves and keeps Santa in Cartier jewelry."

- What is the average amount of time a child spends in Santa's lap at Macy's?
  37 seconds.

- Does Santa ever offer career counseling to children?
  Yes.
  According to Crumpet the Elf of Macy's in New York (as played by David Sedaris), his boss Santa Jerome often recommended the field of entomology to tots because he believed insects have medicinal powers that will one day cure mankind of communicable diseases.

- How many Santas are actually bearded women?
  Approximately 1 percent. (But in response to equal-opportunity pressure, the figure is on the rise, particularly in the striptease Santa field serviced by Take It Off Entertainment, Inc., of Los Angeles and other outlets.)

- Has Nick ever gotten a grown-up request?
  Yes, more than one:
  - In 1986, at Gimbel's in New York, a young man told Santa Sam Cordona, "I want a girl." To which Cordona said, "What do you want a girl for?" The young man's reply: "Santa, *you* know why."
  - In 1992, at Macy's in New York, a six-year-old told Santa: "I want Proctor and Gamble to stop animal testing."
  - Santa Bill Horning from Stateline, Nevada, has this to say about those who sit on his lap in the lobby of Harvey's Casino: "The younger adults ask for fancy cars and money. Middle-agers usually want happiness or diamonds. The Golden Oldies just ask to hit a jackpot or two."
  - In Nike's 1994 Christmas ad, NBA bad boy Dennis Rodman grabbed Santa by the collar and gave his wish list: "I want another championship, an MVP trophy, and a pair of Nike Air-Ups." Santa granted him the Air-Ups after the rebounding champ dangled him from the ceiling.

- Has Nick ever had to save the life of a youngster or oldster?
  Twice:
  - Eleven-year-old Renny Schuffman was in the Los Angeles Panorama Mall waiting to see Santa on Christmas Eve, 1989, when suddenly he inhaled his bubble gum. Panorama Santa Daniel Hobbit leapt from his throne and administered CPR, saving Renny's life. Hobbit was later commended by the American Red Cross.
  - Last season in Manhattan, ten rental Santas were distributing fliers outside the Great American Backrub Shop when suddenly, out in the street, a van struck a bicyclist, Philip Anderson, sixty-three. Seconds later, Anderson, delirious, seeing ten Santas stooped over him, muttered: "Am I in the North Pole?" The bearded men helped load the victim into an ambulance. Said Bill Zanca, the Great American Backrub Shop owner, "When the police arrive, there's ten Santas standing around this guy. Only in New York, right?"

- Who carries liability insurance for Santa?
  The Hartford Group offers a $500,000 policy and also insures
  reindeer. In 1994 CNA Insurance of Chicago introduced an
  Elite Universal Security package plan which covered:
  "Santa, his sleigh, eight-reindeer-powered engine with
  turbo-charged Rudolph, North Pole residence and his vacation condo in Boca."

- Has Nick or an elf ever blown his cool?
  Twice:
  - In 1986, at a shopping mall in Philadelphia, an exhausted
    Santa and his elf tried to punch out early. When tots and
    parents still waiting in line protested angrily, the elf report-
    edly "made an obscene gesture," a melee broke out, and
    police had to restore order.
  - Last season Chip and Lori Crabtree brought their three
    boys to see Santa at the Avenues Mall in Jacksonville,
    Florida. Lori had donned a University of Florida Gators
    sweatshirt for the occasion. Said the man in the red suit:

    "Santa Claus doesn't like Gator fans. Santa Claus
    wishes that Florida State would beat the Gators in the
    Sugar Bowl."

    When Lori told Santa he was being rude, he went on,
    "Lady, if you don't like it, you can get them [the kids] off my
    lap!"

    Chip told Santa he didn't like his attitude. Santa
    jumped off his chair and thumped Chip on the chest. "You
    want to do something about it right now, pal? Right here
    on stage?"

    Chip declined and asked for his money back. Santa had
    to be restrained by mall security and his elves.

All I Need
to Know
I Learned in
Kringlegarten

At the largest Claus academy in the U.S., Western Santa School, students are tutored in such matters as proper pillow placement and beard laundering techniques (with Woolite). The Claus Curriculum also·includes imperative Do's and Don'ts. The Seven Golden Rules in the second category are:

- Don't eat onions, chili peppers, or bean burritos at lunch.
- Don't say "Ho-Ho-Ho!" (It scares kids.)
- Don't promise. Use evasive answers such as "I'll think it over," or "Let's see what old Santa can do."
- Don't borrow money from parents.
- Don't hobnob with other Santas.
- Don't have a Camel with your elves while "feeding the reindeer": the beard is flammable.
- Don't make un-Santa-like remarks (even if bitten, kicked, or "royally christened").

Occupational
Hazards

*By the time Christmas is over, I swear I'll never do it again.
But by the next August I'm singing "Jingle Bells."*
—Matthew Cariton, twenty-six-year-old composer, Macy's New York Santa

Being the Big Guy isn't always a sleigh ride. What do veterans and insiders have to say about the all too common occupational hazards and conditions?

- Santa Sauna Suit : "It's hot enough inside there to grill a cheese sandwich," reports Macy's Santa Matthew Cariton, who lost ten pounds one season.
- Santa knee: A serious dermatological condition difficult to cure, and not always easy to prevent. Advises Adrian Cohen, a trainer at the Western Rent-a-Santa school in New York, "If you get a 'royal christening,' call over your elf immediately."

- Santa-nesia: A loss of memory and/or ability to communicate. Reports Santa Kevin McClosky, thirty, a freelance artist in the off-season, "I would try to say something to my wife, and all I could get out was, 'What is your name?' "

In addition to these and other perils professionals must face, some have encountered threat to beard, belly, and more while dispatching their holiday duty. Here is a brief chronology of Claus calamities.

- 1880, Brooklyn: After one too many eggnogs on Christmas Eve, John Denkler, twenty-eight, decided he was Santa Claus and needed to start deliveries immediately. He jumped out of the second-story window of his house, landed headfirst in a snowbank, and sustained a concussion.
- 1911, New York: On another Christmas Eve, Alderman Frank J. Dotzler, a 375-pound member of the East Side Fat Man's Club, got stuck on a ladder inside a chimney when playing Santa for local kids. The chimney had to be demolished to release Dotzler. Afterward, undaunted, he and two of the smallest East Side Fat Man's Club members—Phil Fecher (240 pounds) and Martin Max (235 pounds)—commandeered a peddler's cart and distributed candy to youngsters.
- 1982, Waterford, Maine: Santa Ronald Bradford dove from a two-engine Cessna sleigh with a sackful of toys. His target: a children's Christmas party in an apartment complex five thousand feet below. His parachute failed to open and at one thousand feet he was heard to exclaim, "Ho-Hoo-HooOO!" Just then his reserve chute opened, much to the merriment of the children and himself.
- 1986, Santa Fe, New Mexico: Volunteer Santa James Stevenson visited the state penitentiary, but hardly had he begun to receive prisoners' kids before the pistol of his elf, Sheriff Dickson Womack, accidentally discharged and winged him.
- 1988, Minneapolis, Minnesota: Santa was persuaded to pose for a photo with a couple's pet chimpanzee at a Dayton mall. When the flash went off, the chimp went ape, ripped off

Santa's beard, attacked the elf with the camera, and lost control of his sphincter. The Dayton North Pole was closed for an hour to clean up after the incontinent chimp.

- 1993, Sacramento, California: While working at the light-rail station, a weekend Santa Claus was the victim of a drive-by shooting. Luckily it was only a gut shot with a pellet gun, and Santa was soon back on his beat. Weeks later, he and his wife led a squadron of police cars and fire engines into the city's gang heartland, the New Helvetia housing project, and distributed candy canes and reconditioned mountain bikes and ten-speeds.

Santa Speak

"Santa Sacroiliac"
Lower lumbar condition caused by repeated
kiddie lifting.

"Go out and feed the reindeer"
Santa milk, cookie, and coffee break.
(Whispered by fresh Santa to Santa-to-be-spelled.)

"Nick Fit"
What happens to an unspelled Claus
too long without a Camel.

"Clausophobia"
Phobic condition suffered by some adults.

"In-Santa-ty Clause"
Temporary craziness that comes at the end of
a trying day or season.

"PMS"
Post-Merriness Syndrome suffered by many Santas.

The Rudolph
Report

Now some important facts and stats about reindeer—regular, as well as winged, with red noses.

- The original name of Rudolph, the Red-Nosed Reindeer, coined by Montgomery Ward adman Robert May:
Rollo or Reginald.
- Number of flying reindeer regularly seen over North Pole, Alaska, on Christmas Eve, according to official North Pole Police records:
10.
- The only reindeer with the ability to fly, according to *Life* magazine (December 1993):
The Peary caribou, or *Rangifer tarandus pearyi*. Reports Peter Lent, U.S. Fish and Wildlife biologist and reindeer expert, "A Peary weighs only 150 pounds and has a phenomenal strength-to-weight ratio."
- Where to ride a real reindeer-driven sleigh:
Santa Claus Village, Arctic Circle, Greenland. Travel pro-

vided by FinnWay Tours. (Other attractions of the North
Pole Trek package: dogsledding; snowmobiling; aurora bore-
alis watching; and cruising on an icebreaker ship.)

- Number of Rudolphs currently leased in southern California
during the holidays by Operation Santa Claus, Inc.:
33.

- Biggest Rudolph athletic event in the U.S.:
Rudolph's Red Nose Run at Nashville Christmas Celebration.

- Most recent reindeer management position open in the U.S.:
1993. The National Parks Service advertised an opening for
a Reindeer Manager (official title: Resource Management
Specialist) at the Bering Land Bridge National Preserve outside Nome, Alaska. Responsibilities included managing
17,000 reindeer that graze on the park's 2.8 million acres.
Salary: $22,925–$34,736 DOE.[10]

- Seasonal festival where reindeer meat is on the menu:
Alaskan Eskimo Christmas Celebration. (Also available: seal
blubber with blueberries.)

- Location of the Rudolph the Red-Nosed Reindeer Restau-
rant:
Santa's Village, Nuuk, Greenland, run by the country's Santa
Foundation.

[10]Source: "For this job, the sleigh bells are optional," USA Today, 12-13-93.

Polito-Claus

Not surprisingly Santa and his reindeer have begun to figure more and more importantly in politics in recent years. Here now, a few questions about key players and events.

1. According to a past *Newsweek* investigative report, "The president typically wears antlers and a red Rudolph nose around the house during the holidays." This president was:
   a. JFK.
   b. LBJ.
   c. Jimmy Carter.
   d. Bill Clinton.
   e. Richard Nixon.

2. In 1970 the Interstate Commerce Commission issued Santa Claus a license to operate a two-runnered, reindeer-powered sleigh. But the license had this conditional clause:
   a. Santa was prohibited from operating the sleigh while under the influence.
   b. He was prohibited from picking up non-elf hitchers.
   c. His sleigh service must result in peace on earth, goodwill to men.

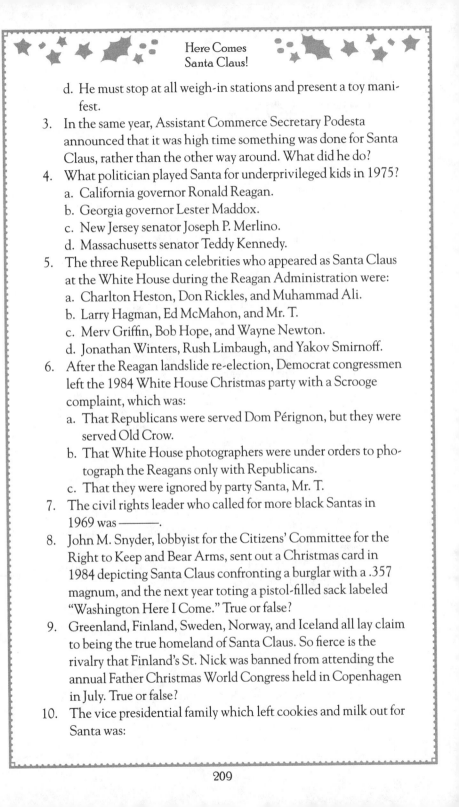

    d. He must stop at all weigh-in stations and present a toy manifest.

3. In the same year, Assistant Commerce Secretary Podesta announced that it was high time something was done for Santa Claus, rather than the other way around. What did he do?

4. What politician played Santa for underprivileged kids in 1975?
    a. California governor Ronald Reagan.
    b. Georgia governor Lester Maddox.
    c. New Jersey senator Joseph P. Merlino.
    d. Massachusetts senator Teddy Kennedy.

5. The three Republican celebrities who appeared as Santa Claus at the White House during the Reagan Administration were:
    a. Charlton Heston, Don Rickles, and Muhammad Ali.
    b. Larry Hagman, Ed McMahon, and Mr. T.
    c. Merv Griffin, Bob Hope, and Wayne Newton.
    d. Jonathan Winters, Rush Limbaugh, and Yakov Smirnoff.

6. After the Reagan landslide re-election, Democrat congressmen left the 1984 White House Christmas party with a Scrooge complaint, which was:
    a. That Republicans were served Dom Pérignon, but they were served Old Crow.
    b. That White House photographers were under orders to photograph the Reagans only with Republicans.
    c. That they were ignored by party Santa, Mr. T.

7. The civil rights leader who called for more black Santas in 1969 was ———.

8. John M. Snyder, lobbyist for the Citizens' Committee for the Right to Keep and Bear Arms, sent out a Christmas card in 1984 depicting Santa Claus confronting a burglar with a .357 magnum, and the next year toting a pistol-filled sack labeled "Washington Here I Come." True or false?

9. Greenland, Finland, Sweden, Norway, and Iceland all lay claim to being the true homeland of Santa Claus. So fierce is the rivalry that Finland's St. Nick was banned from attending the annual Father Christmas World Congress held in Copenhagen in July. True or false?

10. The vice presidential family which left cookies and milk out for Santa was:

a. The Quayles (1990).
b. The Gores (1994).
c. The Fords (1973).
d. The Mondales (1980).

EXTRA CREDIT

- In 1989, George Plimpton was given $10,000 by *Fortune* magazine to play Santa for ten international VIPS. At the top of his list were the Bushes and the Gorbachevs. What surprises did Plimpton come up with for each couple?

ANSWER KEY:

1. d. Bill Clinton.
2. c. His sleigh service must result in peace on earth, goodwill to men.
3. He awarded the town of Santa Claus, Indiana, a grant for $160,000 to help create jobs for the unemployed.
4. c. New Jersey senator Joseph P. Merlino.
   (Georgia governor Lester Maddox played Santa in 1970.)
5. b. Larry Hagman (1985), Ed McMahon (1986), Mr. T. (1984).
6. b. That White House photographers were under orders to photograph the Reagans only with Republicans.
7. Reverend Jesse Jackson.
8. False. Snyder's first card featured a .44 magnum; his second said "California Here I Come."
9. True.
10. b. The Gores (1994). Tipper Gore told *Ladies' Home Journal* last season that at bedtime her kids—Karenna (21), Kristin (17), Sarah (15), Albert III (12)—"open the fireplace grate and leave cookies and milk out for Santa."

Extra Credit:

- The Bushes: a custom-made bronze model of the president on board his Kennebunkport fishing skiff, *Fidelity*, with Barbara and Millie, catching a bluefish.
  The Gorbachevs: an antique "Friendship" quilt from Missouri, and three Stress Relief audiocassettes from Synthetic Research, Inc. ("Night in the Country," "Gentle Rain in Pine Forest," and "Slow Ocean").

The Santa Final Exam

Now, in closing, the semester test on General Clausology:

1. In the old days, other legendary people throughout the world also gave out gifts on Christmas night. Name a few.
2. What did St. Nick use for transportation before Clement Moore gave him Dasher, Dancer, Donder, and the rest of the reindeer in 1823?
3. How many U.S. towns are named Santa Claus?

DOUBLE JEOPARDY

4. In Santa Claus, Georgia, there is no crime, no one locks their doors, and streets are named Dasher, Dancer, Jingle Bells, etc. Last season, a Hollywood studio sent free movie passes to the residents of Santa Claus. The passes were for what popular holiday release:
   a. *Miracle on 34th Street*.
   b. *The Santa Clause*.

c. *Mixed Nuts*.

d. *Dumb and Dumber*.

5. The real U.S. North Pole is located in ———. Its current population is ———. Its five most popular shops are ———.

6. The current price of a deed to a piece of the North Pole is $25, plus postage and handling. True or false?

7. What NFL football star dressed up as Santa for his kids every year until 1991?

a. Boomer Esiason.

b. William "the Refrigerator" Perry.

c. Ice Cube Metcalf.

d. Joe Montana.

e. Neon Deion Sanders.

8. In 1993, Bruce Waldack, president of computer network Digital Nation, said, "We believe strongly that this is Santa's post office of the future." What is the on-line address of this new post office beyond the North Pole?

9. According to the 1994 holiday issue of *Skeptic* magazine, if in fact Santa exists and doesn't short anybody, he has to:

- Fly at 3,000 times the speed of sound (causing sonic booms and risking sleigh meltdown).
- Make 822.6 drops a second to reach every Christian household.
- Carry 321,300 tons of toys (dropping no more than two pounds per stop).
- Employ 1,214,200 reindeer.

True or false?

10. Last season the Thornton Talent Agency, the self-described "No. 1 dwarf agency" in Britain, was called upon to supply little people for Christmas productions of *Snow White and the Seven Dwarfs*. The agency ran into a problem. Said a spokesman: "There is a severe shortage of dwarfs. We have more than sixty-five on our books. They are all booked for Christmas." As a result *Snow White and the Seven Dwarfs* holiday productions:

a. Did not open.

b. Opened with little people working overtime.

c. Opened, using slightly taller people.

d. Opened, using children and cardboard cutouts.

EXTRA CREDIT

- In the old days Santa only had one kind of elf: the all-purpose Workshop Elf. Today the help Santa needs has become far more demanding, requiring diversification. Name some specialist elves who are currently at work in malls and department stores today.

ANSWER KEY:

1. Denmark: Julenissen the Elf. Finland: Wainamoinen and Ukko. Switzerland: St. Lucy. Greece: St. Basil. Italy: Befana. Russia: Baboushka. Bulgaria: Grandfather Koleda. Syria: the Gentle Camel of Jesus. Japan: Santa Kurosu no ojiisan (a.k.a. "Uncle Chimney")
2. A donkey.
3. Three.

Double Jeopardy:

4. b. *The Santa Clause.*
5. Alaska, 20 miles east of Fairbanks, 130 south of Arctic Circle. Population: 15,000. Five most popular shops: North Pole Tanning Salon, Santa's Suds (a laundromat), Santa's Travel, Elf's Den (a tavern/cafe), and Santa Claus House (run by Mike Miller, a member of Alaska House of Representatives, and his sister, Merry Christmas Key).
6. False. The price is $2.50. (Available at the Santa Claus House, North Pole, Alaska. Or by mail order, with SASE.)
7. d. Joe Montana.[11]
8. @csgi.com. Other e-mail addresses: Internet: santa@intacc.net., santa@northpole.net.
9. False. According to *Skeptic* calculations Santa would only need 214,200 reindeer.
10. d. Opened, using children and cardboard cutouts.

---

[11]Before the 1992 season the star quarterback told reporters, "On Christmas Eve, I get dressed up in a Santa Claus suit. Then Jennifer takes Polaroid pictures of me putting things in the kids' stockings. Last year, though, Alexandra said, 'That looks like Daddy.' So this year I'll have to get another Santa up on the roof so they can hear him."

Extra Credit:

- According to Crumpet the Elf, of Macy's New York, "You can be an Entrance Elf, a Water Cooler Elf, a Bridge Elf, Train Elf, Maze Elf, Island Elf, Magic-Window Elf, Emergency-Exit Elf, Counter Elf, Magic-Tree Elf, Pointer Elf, Santa Elf, Photo Elf, Usher Elf, Cash-Register Elf, or Exit Elf."

VII.

Noel Noir

Scrooges, Grinches,
Accountants, Economists,
and a few ACLU Attorneys

Oh! but he was a tight-fisted hand at the grindstone,

Scrooge! a squeezing, grasping, scraping, clutching

old sinner! No warmth could warm, nor wintry weather

chill him. No wind blew bitterer than he, no falling

snow or pelting rain was more intent upon its purpose.

—Charles Dickens, *A Christmas Carol*, of Ebenezer Scrooge

Christmas has become a net loss as a

socio-economic institution. Although for many years

it has been justified on the grounds that it is "merry,"

rigorous quantitative analysis establishes that

the opposite is the case. The holiday is an insidious and

overlooked factor in America's dwindling savings

rates, slack work ethic, and high crime rates. Nor does it

truly fulfill its purported distributional objective.

—James S. Henry, from "Why I Hate Christmas (The Grinch Has It Right),"
The New Republic

The Roots
of Modern
Humbug

E benezer Scrooge wasn't the first to catch the humbug. The Roman emperors were the initial victims. Later the germ spread to the Puritans and Pilgrims. And today the bug seems to reaching epidemic proportions in an otherwise robust American population.

Consider the alarming figures.

In a 1989 national survey, 74 percent of Americans said they felt the true meaning of Christmas had been lost. Only 2 percent said they caroled. And 25 percent admitted to occasionally being in the dumps during the holidays. Psychologists currently estimate that there has been a 100 percent increase in the frequency of the holiday funk since 1948.

In a 1993 USA Today poll[1] adults were asked to compare the fun they have over the holidays now with the fun they remember having as kids: 32 percent said they have about as much fun now, 52 percent said they have less, only 16 percent felt they have more.

Even the popularity of a white Christmas has declined in recent

[1] "Are we having fun yet?" USA Today, 12-27-93.

years. According to a recent ABC News–*Money* magazine survey of five hundred people, 63 percent said they preferred to spend the season somewhere sunny and warm rather than cold and snowy.[2]

Many city offices have become as chilling as Scrooge & Marley's London collecting house. According to a 1989 survey of large firms in New York, 66 percent of employees exchanged no holiday gifts; 33 percent gave poinsettias, desk calendars, and/or food. One firm said its employees' gift would be "keeping their jobs."

Some formerly merry people have succumbed to the adversities of modern living. In 1981 Bob Horek, a.k.a. "Santa Bob," worked his way up from a Detroit Macy's elf to a New York Macy's parade Santa, only to be fired after the parade due to complaints from TV viewers that he was "an effeminate-looking and -acting Santa." Horek didn't ask for his job back, though Macy's said it would rehire him for in-house North Pole work only. "I didn't want to give them the satisfaction of saying Santa is no longer fun for me," said Horek. "They made him a little bit of a Scrooge."[3]

Today not even Zuzu of *It's a Wonderful Life* feels the same as she once did. The real Zuzu, Karolyn Grimes Wilderson, now a retired medical technician from Stilwell, Kansas, went on a national tour of Target department stores during the 1993 season with three other actors who played Jimmy Stewart's children. Afterward *The Washington Post* interviewed her and found her to be "a friendly and casual woman, yet given to occasional sharp comment." Referring to the many angel dolls and rose petals she has received from fans over the years, the former Zuzu told the *Post*, "I've got a box full of crap people've sent me. I mean, gag!"[4]

Even so, in spite of dispiriting cases and statistics, the majority of us still more or less enjoy the holidays. True, we have all come down with a touch of the humbug from time to time, but by and large it is a passing condition. And, as we have learned from *A Christmas Carol*, even the most serious case is reversible if the patient is willing to go into the belly of the beast and take a little hair of the dog that bit him.

On that note now, the history of humbug . . . :

[2] Of the group, 70 percent was over thirty-five years old; 64 percent were married; 65 percent earned less than $50,000 annually.
[3] Source: "The Perils of Santa," *The Wall Street Journal*, 12-8-81.
[4] Source: "Zuzu Has a Wonderful Life After All," *The Washington Post*, 12-25-93.

A Brief History of Humbug

575   Bishop Martin of Bracae forbids use of all greenery and "other dangerous Roman customs." Two hundred years later, Pope Zacharius prohibits Christians from participating in "heathenish" Yule celebration.

1200   Christmas Day: The Prioress of Kirkley bleeds leader of the Merry Men, Robin Hood, to death with leeches.

1214   Christmas Day: A disgruntled mob of barons crashes King John's Yule party at Windsor and demands that he sign a leftist gift certificate called the Magna Carta.

1659   Massachusetts Puritans pass the Five-Shilling Anti-Christmas Law: "Whosoever shall be found observing any such day as Christmas, or the like, either by forbearing of labor, feasting in any other way, shall be fined 5 shillings."

1843   Ebenezer Scrooge is born.

1951   *Scrooge*, the movie, is released, staring Alastair Sim as the the irascible old penny pincher.

1971   Rochester, New York, Police Commissioner Mastrella allows BAH HUMBUG to be sprayed on Public Safety Building windows. Mastrella defends the holiday message, saying "Scrooge is part of Christmas." He tells his critics that no one would have paid attention to the message if it had said "Merry Christmas."

1972   Indianapolis Municipal Court Judge F. L. Harlor releases twenty-six convicted drunk drivers from custody on Christmas Eve; four men say they prefer to to spend the Yule in jail.

1975   Allen Cutcher, grand wizard of the Ebenezer Holiness Church in Longwood, Florida, hangs two Santa Clauses in effigy. (See "The Anti-Clauses," page 226)

1979   ACLU attorney Steven Pevar, representing Roger Lorey, father of kindergartner Justin, argues in U.S. Appeals Court, St. Louis, that Christmas festivity should be banned from public school assemblies. (See "The Crèche and Caroling Wars," page 231)

1980   Seventy-five robed members of the KKK try to crash the Nashville, Tennessee, Christmas parade.

1986   Christmas Day: New York Governor Mario Cuomo rejects a clemency request by Jean S. Harris, serving fifteen years to life for the murder of Dr. Herman Tarnower, creator of the Scarsdale Diet.

1986   The New York Fire Department orders Cartier Jewelers to remove thirty live Christmas trees from its premises, saying they are fire hazards because of the pitch they contain. Ralph Destino, Cartier chairman, denounces Mayor Koch as "Mayor Scrooge."

1990 $3,025 is paid at auction for a 1942 Christmas card signed by Hitler.

1991   Submitting to pressure by landlords, the Milwaukee County Circuit Court, headed by Judge Patrick J. Sheedy, rules that there is no legal basis for delaying Christmas evictions of tenants behind on rent.

1993   "Feeling very strongly" that the Christmas spirit makes juries too lenient, judges of the Mercer Court of Common Pleas in Pennsylvania close their court from mid-December until New Year, even for civil cases.

1993   December 21 is declared National Humbug Day by the Wellness Permission League of New York. Encouraging everyone to vent their holiday frustrations, it prescribes twelve humbugs for Wellness.

1994   SCROOGE (the Society to Curtail Ridiculous, Outrageous and Ostentatious Gift Exchanges) is founded by Chuck Langham of Sunnyvale, California.

How the Good
Guys Stole Back
Christmas

Grinches, scrooges, and spoilsports have abounded from the earliest ages, especially in the political arena. But, despite their strength, the joyful have always triumphed in the end, as we see from this age-by-age replay of the struggle:

PAGAN PERIOD

303   Emperor Diocletian burns twenty-thousand Christian revelers alive in the temple at Nicomedia, Bithynia, for the holidays.

337   Emperor Constantine is baptized on his deathbed, and the first Christmas is officially celebrated in the Roman empire.

PILGRIM & PURITAN

1620   Thomas Jones, master of the *Mayflower*, writes in the ship's log: "At anchor in Plymouth harbor; Christmas Day, but not observed by these colonists, they being opposed to all saints' days . . . A large party went ashore this morning to fell timber and begin building . . . No man rested all that day."

The colonists "have some beere" that evening. The next year, Governor Bradford catches them "at play openly; some pitching the barr and some at stoole-ball, and such like sports."

1643   English Puritan Parliament outlaws Yuletide feasts. Clergyman are imprisoned for preaching on the twenty-fifth. Parish officers of St. Margaret's, Westminster, are fined for decorating the church with rosemary and bay. Riots break out. William Prynne, a Puritan lawyer, publishes an anti-Christmas manifesto, *Histriomastix*, which begins: "Our Christmas lords of Misrule—together with dancing, masques, mummeries, stage-players, and such other Christmas disorders—they should be eternally abominated by all pious Christians!"

1660   King Charles II drives the Puritans from power and restores Yuletide celebration. He arrests Prynne, pillories him, cuts off both his ears, and has his book burned in front of his face. Releasing the attorney, he fines him five thousand pounds, expels him from Oxford University, and disbars him from the legal profession.

THE SIXTIES & SEVENTIES

1969   Castro cancels Caribbean Christmas Celebration during sugar harvests saying, "Cuba cannot afford the luxury of having fiestas."

Cubans have private fiestas anyway.

1972   Thirty-seven protesters, led by Reverend Phillip F. Berrigan, stage a medieval morality play in front of the White House that casts President Nixon as King Herod.

Meanwhile, inside, ignoring the skit, Mrs. Nixon, Julie, and Tricia sing Christmas carols, accompanied by the chief executive on piano.

1975 President Ford receives a holiday card which accuses him of throwing Christmas ski junkets in Vail, Colorado—at taxpayers' expense. The card is signed "Ebenezer Scrooge."

1976–77 The president continues to throw holiday ski junkets at taxpayers' expense.

THE EIGHTIES & NINETIES

1988 Palestinians boycott Christmas in Bethlehem. The holiday cocktail party with Israeli officials is canceled; only five Christmas choirs sing in Manger Square (down from fourteen in 1987); and no Boy Scouts greet the visiting pope. Said an Arabic father, "The children are very sad because there is no Baba Noel."

1993–94 Parties, choirs, and Boy Scouts return to Bethlehem as a result of peace initiatives. Said Nadia Mubarak, a Bethlehem boutique owner, "Business is excellent. People are in good spirits." Nafez Al-Rifai, spokesman of the Fatah branch of the PLO, summed the situation up: "Christ was a Palestinian. Actually Christ was the first martyr. So it *is* a national holiday."

1994 British vicar Dick Haigh writes "Do You Deceive Your Children?" for the December issue of his parish magazine. The article declares: "This month millions of small children will be encouraged to believe in a falsehood, the reality of Father Christmas. At the same time, millions of older children will come to realize that Father Christmas is not to be taken seriously and they have been duped."

The article is denounced by members of Parliament and Haigh is branded a "spoilsport."

Christmas Curmudgeonry: Cigars, French Girls, and Greasy Sausages

My Lord!

I have not yet received the cigars and don't need your gifts. When I get them I'll throw them down the toilet . . .

Three days ago I was at a Christmas party for the insane, held in a violent ward. Too bad you weren't there.

Since the New Year will soon be with us, may I wish your family a Happy New Year and all the best—as for you, may you see Beelzebub in your dreams!

The money has been given to the French girl, the one you like so much, in payment for your immoral conduct with her . . .

All the best, sir. Is everyone well, my good man?

Your, sir,
A. Chekhov
[A letter to his brother-in-law, 1895]

The prospect of Christmas appalls me.
—Evelyn Waugh, 1950

I am sorry to have to introduce the subject of Christmas in these articles. It is an indecent subject; a cruel, gluttonous subject; a drunken, disorderly subject; a wasteful, disastrous subject; a wicked, cadging, lying, filthy, blasphemous, and demoralizing subject. Christmas is forced on a reluctant and disgusted nation by the shopkeepers and the press: in its own merits it would wither and shrivel in the fiery breath of universal hatred; and anyone who looked back to it would be turned into a pillar of greasy sausages.

—George Bernard Shaw, from *Our Theatres in the Nineties*, 1898

It is necessary to factor in all the time spent searching for "just the right gifts," writing and mailing cards to people one ignores the rest of the year, decorating trees, attending dreary holiday parties with highly fattening, cholesterol-rich eggnog drinks and false cheer, and returning presents.

—James S. Henry, economist, from "Why I Hate Christmas (The Grinch Has It Right)," *The New Republic*, 12-31-90

The Anti-Clauses: New Tales of Holiday Terrorists

T he story of Scrooge's haunting by the three Ghosts has been replaced by a new and even spookier generation of holiday tales from Christmas present—all of them true, not one make-believe:

1975, CHRISTMAS EVE, LONGWOOD, FLORIDA: Police issued an APB for two plastic Santas that had been liberated from Allen Cutcher, grand wizard of the Ebenezer Holiness Church. Cutcher had had the figures hanging "in effigy" from a scaffold on his front lawn. At the time of the theft, a flowerpot was also allegedly thrown through Cutcher's front window. Sources close to the Longwood Police Department investigation said that the vandalism and theft was probably the work of Cutcher's neighbors. Later four of them dropped by his house—under police escort—and tried to convince him that hanging Santa "spoils Christmas." Cutcher again demanded the return of his Santas and threatened legal action.

1980, BURLINGTON, NORTH CAROLINA: Some 125 members of Truth Tabernacle Church, led by R. R. Robertson, put a St. Nick doll on trial, found him guilty of fraud, and lynched him.

1984, BURLINGTON, VERMONT: While children were in line at the local mall waiting to see Santa, twenty-five-year-old Brian Pearl burst through the crowd and exclaimed, "There is no such thing!" Pearl was arrested by Burlington police on trespassing charges and taken to jail. His bail was set at $50.

1993, DENVER, COLORADO: In the week before Christmas, eight malls were faxed a Santa death threat, which read in part:

> TIME IS RUNNING OUT ON THAT FATSO. BY THURSDAY, HE WILL BE HISTORY ALONG WITH ANYBODY THAT GETS IN MY WAY. CHUCK E. CHEESE WAS NOTHING COMPARED TO THIS.

Referring to a recent shooting rampage at Chuck E. Cheese, a local pizza restaurant, the note was signed "TERMINATOR XX." Each mall removed its Santa Claus and posted a sign at his chair saying he had returned to the North Pole "on urgent business." Said Lisa Herzlich, marketing director for the Cherry Creek mall, "If I'm going to put a bulletproof vest on Santa and let a kid sit on his lap, my heart just lurches at that thought." On Thursday, December 23, a special SWAT Santa—Guardian Angel Sebastian Metz, flanked by his burly bodyguard elves—received kids at the Denver and Boulder police departments.

The Flipside of the Fatman

There's another side to Santa that can be frightening:
the idea that Santa is all-powerful, that he can see
inside us, that he knows what we are thinking.

—Mister Rogers, interview for *Ladies' Home Journal*, 1988

Loose-fitting nylon beard, fake optical twinkle,
cheap red suit, funny rummy smell…
Something scary and off-key about him, like one
of those Stephen King clowns.

—John Updike, "The Twelve Terrors of Christmas,"
The New Yorker magazine, December 1993

We believe Santa Claus is Satan.

—Allen Cutcher, grand wizard of the Ebenezer Holiness Church, 1986

Nick at
Night Court

W̲e have already seen how, professionally speaking, most Scrooges are either fire-and-brimstoners, writers, economists (Scrooge himself was an accountant), sociopaths, or attorneys such as William Prynne, whose ears Charles II cut off.

Of all these groups, only one has the power to sue, subpoena, or send Santa upriver.

Here is some precedent-setting litigation involving the saint as both plaintiff and defendant in Christmases past to present:

- 1739, London, England: St. Nick is tried on charges of Mischief and Mayhem. Reported a London newspaper: "The trial of old Father Christmas for encouraging his Majesty's subjects in Idleness, Drunkenness, Gaming, Rioting, and all mannyer of Extravagance and Debauchery at the Assizes, was held in the city of Profusion before the Lord Chief Justice Churchman, Mr. Justice Feast."
- 1968, Philadelphia, Pennsylvania: George Mason, Jr., files a $250,000 suit charging that the pay-per-talk Santa Claus his

five-year-old phoned used obscenities during their taped conversation.

- 1975, Omaha, Nebraska: Santa Claus is arrested in a local mall and jailed for failure to pay child support. He pleads for leniency from the court. Judge James O'Brien remands him "to the custody of his elves."
- 1989, San Francisco, California: Santa is tried before the San Francisco Court of Historical Review and Appeal. His gender and discriminatory elf hiring practices are debated.
- 1991, New York, New York: Macy's Santa, Mark Woodley, forty-two, a former architect, sues the department store for firing him after discovering that he is gay and takes Prozac. Macy's argues that the antidepressant drug causes mood swings inappropriate for a Santa. Macy's prevails.
- 1994, Paris, France: A city court cuts the "Father Christmas" phone lines of SB Communications and Editions de l'Eléphant for bilking youngsters.

The Crèche
and Caroling
Wars

The holiday battleground goes well beyond Santas, of course, and now involves the ACLU, federal courts, crèches, and caroling. Here are some highlights of Christmas court from the last decade:

COURT LOG
- 1983, Pawtucket, Rhode Island: The ACLU files suit against Pawtucket township for putting up a Nativity scene. It wins in lower courts. But the U.S. Supreme Court, handing down the "Reindeer Ruling," decides that the nonreligious elements in the Pawtucket display—Santa Claus, reindeer, and elves—diluted its religious content and therefore did not violate separation of church and state laws.
- 1985, Cos Cob, Connecticut: The ACLU files suit against Cos Cob for putting a cross on the firehouse at Christmastime. A federal judge bans the display. In protest, local residents raise crosses on lawns, telephone poles, and rooftops.[5]

[5]In a case to be heard by the U.S. Supreme Court in 1995, however, the ACLU is defending the Ku Klux Klan, who in the 1993 Christmas season was barred from erecting a cross in a Columbus, Ohio, public park.

- 1989, Allegheny County, Pennsylvania: The U.S. Supreme Court rules that the Constitution does not permit Allegheny County to display a Nativity scene with a "Gloria in Excelsis Deo!" sign at its courthouse. But the court allows the display of an eighteen-foot-tall Hanukkah menorah a block away, at Pittsburgh City Hall, next to a forty-five-foot Christmas tree.
- 1991, White Plains, New York: The City Common Council, ending a heated debate over whether to allow a giant electric menorah on parkland, unanimously rejects the display.
- 1994, Antwerp, New York: Vici and Stephen Diehl sue the Congregational Church for broadcasting Christmas carols daily from steeple loudspeakers, five hundred feet from their home. Mrs. Diehl alleges that she has to take medication to stay calm. The state appellate court orders the church to cease and desist with the carols.

The Season's
Greetings Suit

In 1993 the Equal Employment Opportunity Commission filed suit against the Sheraton Chicago Hotel on behalf of telephone switchboard operator Ninette Smith. Ms. Smith alleged that the hotel had violated her religious beliefs.

During the previous December, the hotel had instructed all its operators to answer in-coming calls by saying, "Happy holidays, Sheraton Chicago Hotel and Towers." When on religious grounds Ms. Smith refused, the management told her she could say just "Greetings" if she preferred. But she contended that this too was unacceptable, since she was being asked to do so only during the holiday season.

The suit was resolved when U.S. District Judge James Holderman ruled that saying "Greetings" did indeed violate Ms. Smith's civil rights. The hotel was ordered to pay the plaintiff $1,250 in back salary, plus $2,500 in compensatory damages.

"I feel justice was served," said Smith. "If someone says someone violated their conscience then the employer should respect that."

As for the Sheraton's policy to give employees a paid holiday at Christmastime, a spokesman reported, "Yes, Ms. Smith received holiday pay last year. And, yes, she accepted it."

Humbug Hollywood

Many of the most memorable Scrooges come to us from the entertainment capital. Here is a selection of movie and TV humbugs from Christmases past. Pin the lefthand Scroogism to the right holiday show.

SCROOGISM

MOVIE / TV SHOW

1. "All Rise! The honorable Harold T. Scrooge presiding."

2. "Oh, I got it. You're taking me back to see Christmases Past. I'm getting all goosey and blubbery. Forget it, pal!"

3. "If the FBI found him here [at Christmas dinner], we could all be thrown in the hoozegow!"

A). Queen Elizabeth I, outlawing Christmas. *Blackadder's Christmas Carol*

B). Miles, after finding out that Murphy and the gang are buying office Christmas gifts, in spite of promising not to do so. *Murphy Brown*

C). Bull, announcing the arrival of Judge Stone for Yuletide lawsuit hearings. *Night Court*

4. "You have all the tender sweetness of a seasick crocodile . . . You're a three-decker sauerkraut and toadstool sandwich with arsenic sauce."

D). Archie Bunker, to Edith, demanding that a Vietnam draft dodger leave his dinner table.
All in the Family

5. "Look, Charlie Brown, we all know that Christmas is a big commercial racket. It's run by a big Eastern syndicate!"

E). Neighbor to Clark Griswald, seeing a beacon in the Christmas sky after a sewer explosion.
National Lampoon's Christmas Vacation

6. "I refuse to buy presents! I refuse to give in! Even if I'm the only one. I'm Miles Silverberg! I'm the boss! . . . The Jewish boss."

F). Carla, before giving a present to her boss, Rebecca, whom she hates.
Cheers

7. "It's a Christmas tradition, Sam. It's called kissing up."

G). "Brother Santa," crashing a Kwanzaa Christmas party, strapped with dynamite.
Martin

8. "He climbs up the chimney, that fat piece of dung. He mooned me two times, he stuck out his tongue. And I heard him explain as he broke wind with glee: You're married with children, you'll never be free."

H). Scrooge Bill Murray to a New York cabbie whose license reads "Spirit of Christmas Past." [Murray is a TV exec producing an X-rated version of *A Christmas Carol*, featuring gymnast Mary Lou Retton as Tiny Tim.]
Scrooged

9. "That ain't the Christmas star, Griz. That's the light at the sewer plant."

I). A public announcement after the Halloweentown King is shot down, and Santa is imprisoned by

Mr. Oogie Boogie.
The Nightmare Before Christmas

10. "You better do what I say or I turn this Christmas into the Fourth of July—ho-ho-HO!"

J). Al Bundy reciting his version of " 'Twas the Night Before Christmas" to kids he has taken hostage in his shoe store.
Married with Children

11. "Although the impostor has been shot down, there is no sign of Santa Claus. Christmas will be canceled this year."

K). Lucy to Charlie Brown, who thinks he's the only one who gets depressed during the holidays.
A Charlie Brown Christmas

12. "I ought to block up the chimneys, burn all the crackers, and kill anyone I see carrying a present."

L). Description of the Grinch.
How the Grinch Stole Christmas

ANSWER KEY:
1. C. *Night Court.*
2. H. *Scrooged.*
3. D. *All in the Family.*
4. L. *How the Grinch Stole Christmas.*
5. K. *A Charlie Brown Christmas.*
6. B. *Murphy Brown.*
7. F. *Cheers.*
8. J. *Married with Children.*
9. E. *National Lampoon's Christmas Vacation.*
10. G. *Martin.*
11. I. *The Nightmare Before Christmas.*
12. A. *Blackadder's Christmas Carol.*

A Gallery
of Real-Life
Grinches

We put only the stuff we want stolen in front.
—A salesman at Gianni Versace boutique to *The New Yorker* magazine,
Christmastime 1994

As the record shows, the pilfering of Christmas pies was common in the sixteenth and seventeenth centuries.

Now, in Christmas present, more than just pies are being snatched.

December is the peak month for theft in the U.S. In 1989, the FBI listed 54,000 robberies and 136,000 auto thefts in its Uniform Crime Report. In 1987, shoplifting reached 2.2 percent of gross holiday sales for department stores nationwide, up 29 percent from 1986. The figures have risen dramatically since then.

Christmas tree theft has been particularly high for some time. In 1975 the U.S. Forest Service reported that organized tree-theft rings had become so extensive that young forests were being blighted. Losses soon became so severe that many state transportation departments began spraying roadside evergreens with repellents during the holiday season.

Christmas tree poaching in the Soviet Union reached epidemic proportions in 1974. Every fourth tree in Moscow was said to have come from bootleggers. Organized gangs spirited firs and spruces into the city strapped under cars, stuffed inside ski bags, and hidden in locomotives. In spite of 22 to 75 ruble ($30 to $100) tree-trafficking fines, the contraband flowed almost unchecked into the snowbound Communist capital. It continued to do so in future seasons and elsewhere in Eastern Europe. The Czech police reported some 500,000 trees poached annually during the same period.

Here now, some documented grinch hits and busts in the U.S.:

- 1974, Nevada City, California: Operation Christmas, founded by Vietnam vet Douglas Allan, is set to ship 5,100 trees to servicemen overseas. Half the shipment, value estimated at $17,500, is stolen.
- 1975 Salt Lake City, Utah: Vernon Black, Richard Spier, Gary Puffer, and Wayne Adams are caught with 276 hot trees. Judge Willis Ritter fines them $30,000, and sentences each to ten years in jail.
- 1975, Boulder, Colorado: Five men and a juvenile are arrested for liberating more than 3,000 Christmas trees from Rocky Mountain National Park.
- 1984, Denver, Colorado: Poachers cause a traffic jam when they scalp more than 10,000 trees in Arapaho and Roosevelt national forests on a holiday weekend.
- 1989, Los Angeles, California: On the night of December 7, someone stole into the front yard of Ricardo Hernandez, a thirty-six-year-old welder, and cut down his twelve-foot Monterey pine decorated with more than 200 lights and 50 ornaments. The next morning, Hernandez and two policemen followed a trail of needles to a nearby apartment. There they found an elderly man, his six grandchildren, and the twelve-foot pine. The man explained that he had purchased the tree "for $7 from a wino."

   Not wanting to spoil the holiday for the man's grandchildren, Hernandez let them keep the tree. When he returned home empty-handed, his daughters Ruth, nine, Xochilt, eight, and Xylina, two, were in tears.

   "I tried to convince them that they couldn't steal the Christmas spirit," Hernandez told the *Los Angeles Times*. "I tried to tell them that they can steal a tree, but not the spirit."

Grinches & Scrooges: The Morning After

I n the end, as we know, the Spirits of Christmas got the best of "that squeezing, grasping, scraping, clutching old sinner." On the morning of the twenty-fifth, not only did Scrooge jump for joy— "A Merry Christmas to everybody! Whoop! Hallo!"—he bought a prize turkey for the Cratchits, he had dinner with his nephew Fred, then he gave his clerk Bob a raise.

As for the Grinch, when the Who's discovered that their Christmas had been stolen and didn't cry "boo-who," but sang carols instead, it finally dawned on the Grinch that Christmas "doesn't come from a store . . . but perhaps means a little bit more." His heart suddenly grew three sizes, he became "as strong as ten Grinches— plus two," he sleighed all the stolen presents back to Whoville, and he had a spirited celebration with the Who's.

And like Scrooge and the Grinch, many seeming hard hearts today have had miraculous turnarounds during the holiday season:

PUPPY RETURN

1973, RANCHO CALIFORNIA, CALIFORNIA: A burglar stole a puppy from the home of John and Alice Hutto during the holiday season. But by Christmas Day he returned the puppy to the Hattos, apologized, and explained that he'd taken it as a gift for his kids. Then he told the couple to lock their doors in the future to avoid more serious burglaries.

BABY JESUS RETURN

1984, BARRINGTON, RHODE ISLAND: On Christmas Day a statue of the Christ child was liberated from a Nativity scene at town hall. Days later it was shipped back by Priority Air from New York.

CAMEL RETURN

1990, MEMPHIS, TENNESSEE: When cardboard cutout manger animals were stolen from the University Christian Church Nativity scene, parishioners made a public appeal for their return. The next morning, a camel and donkey were found propped up on the church lawn. The camel bore this scribbled message: "Sorry 'bout this . . . but I reckon it's the thought that counts. Merry Christmas to all of you."

IRA TERRORIST RETURN

1993, BELFAST, IRELAND: Continuing a forty-five-year tradition, Northern Ireland released 336 prisoners on a seven-day Christmas furlough. Some were "ODCs" ("ordinary decent criminals"); others unaffiliated opponents to British rule; others were IRA terrorists.[6] The last group included Thomas "Wee Tom" McMahon, convicted assassin of Lord Mountbatten; and Robert "Basher" Bates, serving

---

[6]A similar Christmas furlough program has been at work in England and Wales for many years. In 1993, according to the *Baltimore Sun*, "About 1,000 prisoners, including murderers, rapists and armed robbers, were furloughed. Several minimum-security prisons shut down and sent everybody home. British prison officials expect 94 percent will be back on time. Most of the rest will merely be late."

fourteen life terms as one of the "Shankill Butchers" who used meat cleavers on victims. Everyone returned peaceably to lockup after the holidays.

FLAVOR FLAV PEACEMAKER

1993, TEANECK, NEW JERSEY: Star gangsta rapper Flavor Flav broke up a brawl that erupted at a celebrity Christmas party at The Saint's Cafe. The trouble started when guests dissed Ed Loverm, host of cable program *Yo! MTV Raps*, and singer Big Bub. Flavor interceded, seizing Loverm's microphone. "It's Christmas! There's no need for everybody acting wild. This is a joyous day!" (Months earlier, Flavor had been charged with attempted murder for shooting a man he accused of having sex with his girlfriend, whom he had assaulted in 1991, for which he served twenty days in the Nassau County Jail.)

SNOOP DOGGY DOGG OR MR. ROGERS?

1993, WATTS, CALIFORNIA: Star gangsta rapper Snoop Doggy Dogg (a.k.a. Calvin Broadus), on bail for murder, visited Martin Luther King, Jr., Medical Center on December 22, signed autographs, played video games with the patients, and passed out presents to kids.[7]

NONDEDUCTIBLE DONATION

1993, LANCASTER, CALIFORNIA: On Christmas Eve a burglar robbed a local bank of $5,000 and, on his way out to a getaway car, donated $1 to a Salvation Army representative.

---

[7]The day before, the National Political Congress of Black Women staged a demonstration outside the Wiz record store in Washington, D.C., in protest of Snoop Doggy Dogg's album *Doggystyle* and other gangsta rap. "We are trying to get every preacher to speak against this on Christmas," said spokeswoman Nadine Winter. "Our women are queens, not 'ho's or bitches.'" Ms. Winter, Dick Gregory, and others were arrested and carried away in plastic handcuffs.

Yule Capsule: Pounding Smith &
Wessons into Plowshares

In the last few holiday seasons the police departments in both Los Angeles and New York have sponsored gun swap meets. In 1993, the New York event took place at the Washington Heights precinct: 310 weapons, including Uzi submachine guns, were traded for $100 Toys "R" Us gift certificates. The event was so successful that the NYPD ran out of certificates and had to issue IOUs. In Los Angeles 402 weapons were exchanged for Ticketmaster passes to upcoming sporting events and rock concerts. Weapons were melted down into manhole covers.

Book 'em,
Santo![8]

In his red woolen suit, all 325 pounds of him—he looks like Santa Claus; with his deep Ho-Ho-Ho—he sounds like Santa Claus; and hefting a bag stuffed with candy canes—he carries on like Santa Claus.

But who is he really?

Sergeant Pat Martin, booking officer at the Sacramento, California, County Jail.

Since 1986 Martin has been coming to work as Santa during the holiday season. The candy canes he hands out to jail employees and the visiting children of inmates come compliments of the County Deputy Sheriffs' Association. "I try to put some Christmas spirit in the people who kind of walk around with a bah-humbug attitude," says Martin. "Being cops, they have to see the bad side of life all the time."

Does the booking officer in red have a favorite line for incoming felons during the holiday season?

"Sure," he says. "I tell them—'Hey, see! You gotta be good all the time because Santa knows who's naughty and nice!'"

[8]Source: "St. Nick Not Just Up on the Housetop Lately," *Sacramento Bee*, 12-25-93.

Xmas Extra!
The Man in the Chimney

1982, Bossier City, Louisiana: Attempting to enter a well-secured house without activating the burglar alarm, a man climbed up to the roof and jumped down the chimney. But he got stuck—for six hours. Finally the neighbors, hearing muffled cries from the next-door rooftop, called 911. When the police arrived, the man in the chimney reportedly began to holler "Ho-Ho-Ho!" The officers extricated the suspect and arrested him on charges of attempted burglary.

The Humbug Finale

1. Before being visited by Marley and the three spirits, Scrooge tells his nephew Fred:
   "If I could work my will, every idiot who goes about with 'Merry Christmas' on his lips should be boiled with his own ————, and buried with a stake of ———— through his heart!"

2. Besides "Bah Humbug!" what is Scrooge's other favorite holiday saying.
   a. Rubbish!
   b. Hells bells!
   c. Jesus, Mary, and Joseph!
   d. Pooh pooh!

3. The spirit who upset Scrooge the worst and got to the root of his condition was:
   a. Spirit of Christmas Past when showing him his former fiancée, whom he abandoned for love of money.
   b. Spirit of Christmas Present, who showed him the dying Tiny Tim.
   c. Spirit of Christmas Future, who showed him his own grave "overrun by weeds."

4. The most popular of the many sequels of *A Christmas Carol* was the anonymously written *Christmas Eve* (1870). According to this story, what happens to Scrooge?

5. In 1990 economist James S. Henry penned the NeoScrooge platform in "Why I Hate Christmas (The Grinch Has It Right)." What are the five reasons he gives for calling Christmas a "primitive Keynesianism gone awry" and hating it?

6. What horror film drew protests because the ax-murderer in it disguised himself as Santa Claus?
   a. *Deep Red: The Hatchet Murders.*
   b. *The Nightmare Before Christmas.*
   c. *Silent Night, Deadly Night.*
   d. *A Christmas to Remember.*

DOUBLE JEOPARDY

7. In what hit holiday movie did a ten-year-old mobilize "Operation Ho-Ho-Ho" on two burglars attempting to rob a New York toy store—an operation in which he stones them, staple guns them, turpentines them, and electrocutes them with a portable generator?
   a. *Trouble in Paradise.*
   b. *Home Alone 2.*
   c. *Child's Play 2.*
   d. *It's a Wonderful Life.*

8. "You can tell we are in the holiday season because they're starting to use that very festive red-and-green color for the chalk body outlines." Who said it?
   a. Howard Stern.
   b. Jay Leno.
   c. David Letterman.
   d. Dennis Miller.

9. The Grinch's voice in "How the Grinch Stole Christmas" was:
   a. Boris Karloff's.
   b. Lon Chaney, Jr.'s.
   c. Vincent Price's.
   d. Danny DeVito's.

10. What were the three words that best described the Grinch? Why?

EXTRA CREDIT

- After all these years, has a real, live Grinch finally surrendered to the spirit of the season, come clean, and given back Christmas with apologies and a gentleman's handshake?

ANSWER KEY:

1. Pudding; Holly.
2. d. Pooh pooh!
3. a. Spirit of Christmas Past when showing him his former fiancée, whom he abandoned for love of money. ("Spirit, show me no more!" cried Scrooge. "Why do you delight to torture me?")
4. He retires to the country with the Cratchits and, in the end, dies in the arms of Tiny Tim (described as "tiny no longer").
5. Why Henry Hates Christmas:
   - Christmas consumes vast resources in the dubious and uncharitable activity of forced giving.
   - Christmas introduces sharp seasonal fluctuations into the money demand.
   - Christmas leads to a sharp rise in absenteeism and a slump in labor productivity.
   - Christmas is one of the most hazardous times of the year.
   - Excessive eating and drinking are used to compensate for the tribulations of Christmas.
6. c. *Silent Night, Deadly Night* (1984). Due to protest, the movie was pulled from theaters within a few days of opening.

Double Jeopardy:

7. b. *Home Alone 2.*
8. c. David Letterman.
9. a. Boris Karloff's.
10. "STINK, STANK, STUNK." The Grinch's "heart was full of unwashed socks."

Extra Credit:

- Yes, the Grinch came clean. In closing, here is the amazing but true story . . .

The Grinch Comes Clean[9]

One Christmas a man from Wichita, Kansas, found himself without a tree. So he went to the Pawnee Prairie Municipal Golf Course, chopped one down, and, on his way out, he liberated a garden hose too.

Years later, on Christmas Eve, Stan Shaver, the pro at the Pawnee Prairie Golf Club, got a phone call. At first there was no voice on the other end. Shaver assumed it was somebody having second thoughts about a lesson or a tee-off time. Finally, the caller told him he cut a Christmas tree on the golf course in 1973, and had taken a garden hose too.

"I was broke," the man told Shaver. "How much do I owe you? What'll you take?"

"I couldn't give you a figure on it," said the pro, "it's twenty years ago. I'd just say forget about the tree and send me $20."

Soon enough, a man walked into the pro shop, identified himself as the party who had called, gave Shaver $40, chatted with him briefly, then shook his hand and left without giving his name.

"It had been chewing on the guy," said Shaver. "After all those years he finally told his wife, and she told him, 'Go make restitution.' So he did. I thought it was really something."

And with that—

Happy Christmas to all! and to all a good night!

[9]Source: "Christmas Tree Is All Paid Up, 20 Years Later," Associated Press, 12-26-93.

Index